Embracing the Waves

How I survived incomprehensible loss and relearned how to live

JOHN T. CHARTIER

ISBN: 978-0-578-82690-5

Author: John Chartier

Writing Coach: Kim St. Clair

Editors: Jordyn Chartier, Rhonda Chartier, Jean Boles, David James

Copy Editor: Susan Harbin

Cover Designer: David James

Printed in the United States of America

I dedicate this book to Rhonda, my wife and soulmate. You have stayed the course with unwavering love for me, even when I was unlovable. I'm grateful for our beautiful children, Brandon and Jordyn, and the fierce way you have loved and protected them. You showed me how to be a better man and father by living with passion and authenticity. I'm amazed by how you continue to help me grow, and I look forward to our next chapter together. Thank you, my love, for being the best part of every line in my story.

Contents

ACKNOWLEDGMENTS

This book could not have been written had it not been for all of you who helped and encouraged me through the incredible journey of reclaiming my life. *You know who you are.* I will forever remember you with love and gratitude. I hope that my story will encourage others — who may be suffering as I did — to have the courage and discipline to remain steadfast in their pursuit of life. May they also be blessed with people like you to help and encourage them along the way.

FOREWORD

The idea for this book began as I sat in the hospital listening to John share his story with me and my husband for the first time. He could only move his mouth and eyes, yet he brought the details of his accident to life while reassuring us he would be fine. He was doing a "John." He made sure we were okay even though he was suffering. He read the room, saw our distress, and made us laugh.

Rhonda was equally amazing. I remember watching her care for John with her usual humor, even though I knew her heartbreak from our phone conversations. She was just so thankful John was still alive and with her. The power of her will to help him recover was like electricity in the room. You could feel her love for him.

On the six-hour drive back to New Jersey, we were both quiet as we processed what John and Rhonda were facing. We had recently moved away from our home in Ohio, and we wondered how we could support our friends from a distance. In our old lives, we would have helped with yard work and meals. We would have taken shifts at the hospital. We realized that we could not even support John with phone calls at that point of his recovery. We realized that our feelings of powerlessness were magnified a million times for our friends, and we grieved for all they were suffering.

As a clinical mental health counselor who specializes in treating trauma and PTSD, I knew the psychological effects of the accident would be significant for both. Based on the stories I knew from their past, I understood that they were both strong people. I hoped that they could find healing from this trauma as well.

As time passed and John slowly regained some function, I realized that it would be beneficial for him and other people to have a written record of his journey. I hoped that exploring the painful events from his childhood would reveal how he had grown into the resilient person he is today, which led me to talk to him about writing this book. I knew what he had endured, and I knew who he had become.

John's decision to be vulnerable on these pages is, again, just John doing a "John." He will not allow you to feel hopeless or alone. He will be authentic. He will tell you the truth. The dark stuff. The stuff that other people want to hide because they fear appearing weak. And he will tell you the goofy things and the wonderful things. He will tell you the whole story. And above all else, he will make sure you have hope because he believes that this life is a gift and that if you have breath, there is always a story to tell, a laugh to share, and a way to enjoy the moment.

Kim St. Clair

PROLOGUE

"I don't know about you, but I have a lot of mess in my life."
— *Johnny Wimbrey*

In his video titled, *Don't Give Up*, motivational speaker Johnny Wimbrey said, "I don't know about you, but I have a lot of mess in my life. There is no question that my *mess* has now become my message." Stunning words for me to recall as I contemplated writing a book about my accident. For so many of us, we live our lives making assumptions about what will occur, and then when something unexpected happens, we lose our way. We lose hope. I hope that anyone reading this book will be encouraged by my story and find a way to make their *mess* into something meaningful.

My mess started on March 27, 2013, when a wave crashed down on me, broke my neck, and left me paralyzed. The ensuing experiences have led me on a path that has changed me. It's hard to explain, but I feel more fully alive now than I ever have. I've learned to fight to maintain my zeal for life no matter what happens and to find the preciousness of every moment — in the moment. I know that life is a gift.

Occasionally, people tell me how lucky I am when they hear my story or see me for the first time since the accident. People say things like, "Wow, John, you are lucky to be alive!" or "You are so lucky you can walk," and a favorite, "You should be thankful you can feed yourself." The keyword here is "lucky."

I understand the sentiments because I know people want to express their understanding of my injury and acknowledge my progress. Regardless of the sentiment, I have to admit that those words can at times be difficult to hear because "lucky" makes the losses both my family and I have experienced feel insignificant. It can feel like they are saying that "luck" is why I am alive or have the body functions I currently possess. The word "lucky" also minimizes the extreme amount of work put into my recovery.

In our regular lives, we rarely walk up to someone and say they are lucky to walk, feed themselves and live. Are we lucky to function? Yes, we are lucky to function, but most of us wake up each day assuming that those three things will happen without complication.

I know that every bit of function I have is a gift. I also know what I have lost, and I have learned to be grateful while still experiencing complex emotions and grief. Our feelings of powerlessness are magnified as a result. I am extremely grateful to be alive and have regained the function level that I now have, but I am not ignoring this equation's painful side. *Grateful* is a word that can encompass the full range of my emotions. So, it is with gratitude that I tell you my story.

CHAPTER 1
Defining Moments

"In life, we don't usually get to choose the time of our defining moments. We just have to stand and face them when they come..."

— *Darren Shan*

There are moments in our lives that change us forever. For me, that moment came when I suddenly found myself face down on the bottom of the ocean floor, unable to move. I can still clearly see it as if it is frozen in time. Beams of light. Tropical fish. The absence of sound. The absence of breath. Paralysis.

If you had told me what was to come when we were leaving cold, snowy Ohio, I would not have believed you.

On Friday night, March 22, 2013, my wife Rhonda, myself, our friends Ron and Hope, their daughter Kelsey and her friend Heather drove through the night in a rented minivan to Florida to board a cruise ship bound for the Bahamas. I remember driving as the sun rose above the horizon; my whole face broke out into a smile. The brightness and warmth melted away the stress I had left behind at my job. "Hello, sun, my old friend! I'm expecting to spend lots of time with you over the next week!"

Four days later, in Nassau, Bahamas, my smile was even brighter! I stood in the soft, white sand as the rolling waves shimmered blue, inviting me to come and play. It was a gorgeous day at the beach, and Ron and I accepted the invitation and dove into the Atlantic Ocean. We swam for a while until I decided to turn around and join my wife Rhonda back on the beach, where she sat reading.

That decision, to turn back when I did, was as insignificant as any of the other countless decisions we make in a day. I was tired, nothing more, so I turned and waded through the water toward the beach. The sand beneath my feet sunk deeper with each step. Walking became a bit of a struggle, and I stumbled at the exact moment a large wave crashed down on me from behind, plunging my head toward the ocean floor. I face-planted into the sand as the cresting of the large wave caught my legs and took them toward my head, breaking my neck. My seemingly insignificant decision changed everything in my life.

How did we get here?

To fully understand the magnitude of this experience, I think it's important to share a few details of my life before this moment. Living in a small town forty-five minutes outside Cleveland, Ohio, I always enjoyed excellent health. I never really gave my physical abilities much thought. I had a previous health scare in

2010 and didn't want to take anything else for granted.

In May of 2010, I had become sick and couldn't shake it. I developed an upper respiratory illness that hit me hard. My primary care physician diagnosed me with bronchitis and prescribed a strong antibiotic and a cough suppressant, yet I continued to get worse. With a constant cough and overall weakness, I returned to my doctor for a follow-up appointment. He believed my breathing problems were still consistent with bronchitis and gave me an even stronger antibiotic, coupled with a nebulizer to open my breathing passages. He also suggested that I stay home from work for a week to get as much rest as possible.

Although I followed his recommendations, I was feeling even worse by midweek, so I called my doctor again. He told me to continue the antibiotics and assured me I would see a difference within a couple of days. He was right, I did feel better for the next few days, but I could not sleep by the end of the week. When I laid down, I felt like I was hyperventilating, and I could not catch my breath. When I sat up in bed, I could get my breathing under control, but the moment I laid back down, I struggled for breath again.

I attempted to lie down three or four times until I finally went into the living room and sat up watching television until Rhonda woke up and came into the room to find me. By that point, I was concerned and told her I needed to go to the emergency room. It was a sunny spring morning, and the hospital was the last place

I wanted to spend the day, but this was more than me not feeling well — I knew something was wrong.

Once I was seen in the ER, I explained my illness and current treatment to the staff. They attempted to help me, but after two hours, I still had no relief. At that point, I remembered to tell the doctor that my feet had been swollen two nights earlier but that I had thought little about it since the swelling was gone. He found this detail to be particularly important. Bringing the stethoscope back to my chest and listening intently for a long time, he said, "I didn't catch this earlier. How long have you had a heart murmur?" I was completely unaware of having a heart murmur, which surprised him. He left the room to review my tests and came back with a new diagnosis of congestive heart failure. I had fluid on my lungs and lots of it. I was given a diuretic to take those fluids off. Within an hour, the fluids were gone and so was the coughing. I felt great!

My quick response to the diuretic made Rhonda and me begin to doubt the doctor's diagnosis of congestive heart failure based on prior negative experiences at this small regional hospital. We were ready to go home and assumed we could just follow up with my doctor the next day. We did not understand the seriousness of the situation and were surprised when the ER doctor said that I needed to be admitted to the hospital to be monitored overnight until a cardiologist could do an evaluation.

I was stunned that they were admitting me, but I still did not grasp the seriousness of my situation until the next morning when we met with the hospital's cardiologist. He ran many tests, including an echocardiogram and a cardiac catheterization, confirming heart failure. Upon reviewing the test results, the cardiologist said that I needed much more than their hospital could handle. He recommended I be transferred to the Cleveland Clinic to find the underlying cause. Based on my age and overall good health, my test results were very unusual. We agreed to his recommendation and Rhonda said she would drive me to the Cleveland Clinic.

The cardiologist looked at us in disbelief, like we were not getting it at all, and he told us that driving me there was not an option. He had already secured an ambulance for transport and was in my room to make sure I was stable enough for the trip before discharging me for transfer.

From that moment, things happened quickly. Phone calls made. Plans canceled. And then I was in an ambulance on my way to the Cleveland Clinic.

Upon our arrival, I was astonished by the size of the hospital campus. It seemed as if we traveled a mile through hallways and corridors just to get to my room, where I soon met my attending physician. He explained that his entire team would be coming to see me later in the day, and as the hours passed, a steady stream of doctors entered my room and evaluated me.

My primary doctor explained the initial results to help us understand what the treatment team was looking at regarding my diagnosis and treatment. He sat down next to my bed, surrounded by his entire team, and explained that I had an undetected congenital heart condition. The cause of my cardiac distress was a malformed aortic heart valve.

The aortic valve is a one-way valve between the heart and the aorta, the main artery from the heart that distributes oxygen-rich blood to the body. In a normal heart, the aortic valve has three small flaps or leaflets that open widely and close securely to regulate blood flow, allowing blood to flow from the heart to the aorta and preventing blood from flowing backward into the heart. My valve was a bicuspid valve instead of a tricuspid valve. In bicuspid aortic valve disease (BAVD), the valve has only two leaflets. The valve doesn't function perfectly with this deformity, but it may function adequately for years without causing symptoms or obvious signs of a problem.

My doctor told me that the treatment options were either an aortic valve replacement or a complete heart transplant, depending on the tests they were conducting. I had no known history of heart problems, so I had no baseline to understand what any of it meant. *Could this be happening and not a dream?*

Waiting for Answers, Wondering What's Next...

Time moved slowly as we waited for this rigorous evaluation protocol to end and for answers to come. Finally, Rhonda and I were invited to meet with the entire heart replacement team at the Cleveland Clinic to hear their thoughts on my case. One by one, the team walked into my room and introduced themselves and their faces revealed the seriousness of my condition. After the introductions, the lead doctor explained that the two existing aortic valve flaps were oversized, but the missing third flap left a gap that allowed blood to leak and made my heart work overtime. I still didn't comprehend how dangerous the defect was, and I explained that I was playing softball just a week before my initial symptoms. Reality sunk in when one of the doctors told me I was truly fortunate not to have collapsed and died on the ballfield. He explained that I was lucky to have lived to be 48 years old with the decline of my heart function without having an incident. I needed surgery immediately.

Rhonda and I were stunned. The surgical team presented all the facts, asking us to discuss the options and to make a decision. The major concern regarding valve replacement was the threat of dying during surgery based on the low level of heart function I was already experiencing. This danger led the team to consider whether a total heart replacement would be better to increase the odds of survival.

This news shocked us. The doctors shared all the risks as they worked together, evaluating me moment by moment. After much consideration, their final recommendation was to have a valve replacement followed up with rest and medication, hoping that my heart would respond and get stronger. If my heart didn't get stronger, I would be on the waiting list for a heart transplant. We decided to go with their recommendation and have my valve replaced immediately, even with the risk of death during surgery.

The next decision was whether to have a tissue valve, including human or animal tissue — or a mechanical valve. So many choices! The doctors explained both valves in great detail, including the advantages and disadvantages. I chose a tissue valve instead of a mechanical valve. I was told that I would not need future surgery with a mechanical valve but would need to take blood thinners for the rest of my life. They also explained that a mechanical valve makes a slight clicking noise each time it opens and closes. I didn't want to take blood thinners or hear a click every time the valve opened and closed. I am very sensitive to noise and knew constant clicking would aggravate me. I was informed that the tissue valve would eventually wear out and require replacement, but it felt like this was the right decision. I had no idea how important not being on blood thinners would be in the near future!

On the day of surgery, our minister and many of our friends and family, some traveling long distances, came to the hospital to be with me. It was comforting to be surrounded by their love and support and great to know Rhonda wouldn't be alone through this long procedure. I went into surgery, not knowing if I would live, but I felt at peace having said my goodbyes. Rhonda and I had talked about the possibilities the night before and had hope that all would go well, but either way, we believed we would see each other again someday. As I lay there in the hospital bed, I took those moments with everyone in the room and made a mental picture in my brain. The mood was light as we talked about other things rather than the procedure that would soon take place. Their smiles and presence made me feel incredibly valued. I felt honored to be encircled by them before being taken away and prepped for surgery.

My treatment team accompanied me on the trip to the operating room, answering all my questions and concerns, and allowing me to joke with them and alleviate some of my tension. I cannot explain how refreshing that moment was to laugh with them and to feel human as they asked me questions and listened to what I needed to say to them. I felt like a person, not a case or a number. They saw me as a man with a life and emotions, not just a one-dimension summation of test results indicating the need for a valve replacement. It felt good to go into surgery knowing they cared about me as they began the delicate operation that would save my life.

My next memory is waking up in the Intensive Care Unit (ICU) experiencing intense pain with a tube down my throat and wires everywhere, making communication difficult. To make matters worse, my right eye burned, constantly watered and was blurry to see out of. Without being able to speak, it took a while to get Rhonda, my daughter Jordyn, my sisters Diane and Cherie to understand why I kept pointing at my eye and blinking. I guess I'm not exceptionally good at the game of charades. Apparently, my eye was abraded from surgical tape.

It's a foggy memory, but my ventilator tube was removed on the second day, and it felt so good to have that tubing taken out. The excitement for me was finally being able to talk again — or so I thought. I was given ice chips to melt in my mouth, soothing my sore throat from the insertion and extraction of the ventilator tube. Unfortunately, the good feeling didn't last long because I had to get right to work to make sure I could breathe well on my own. My Intensive Care nurse told me that I needed to practice taking deep breaths to help open my airways and prevent fluid from building up in the lungs. She gave me a device and instructed me to put my lips around it, take in a deep breath, and then blow into the tube. It would measure my effort.

I did as she said and by the third inhale, I felt a sharp pain in my back that became so intense that it led to a crisis point when I could no longer breathe. With each inhale, a sharp stabbing pain radiated in my lungs until I could not go on because the pain was unbearable. The doctors rushed in and sedated me to slow down my breathing and I slipped into a twilight state. My body felt no pain at this point, but I could hear people talking faintly in the room around me. I thought I was back in surgery because I could hear people speaking as my body was being moved. Hours later, when I awoke from the sedation, Rhonda stood by my side, and I asked her what was done to me. "Nothing," was Rhonda's reply, but I didn't believe her. I was sure that I had undergone another surgery and couldn't be persuaded otherwise, causing frustration for my already confused mind.

ICU was a lonely place for me, and I felt disconnected from everyone because I was isolated for much of the day. The window of time allotted for visitation was minimal and reserved for immediate family. I felt broken and lost, but Rhonda remained strong, staying by my side whenever she was allowed in the room. I never saw her fear through her smiles and encouragement. ICU is a painful blurred memory for me, but she experienced each agonizing second fully aware of the possibilities while waiting for my prognosis.

Rhonda told me later that sometimes she would just go in the hallway, and with her back to the wall, she would slide to the floor and break down, crying until she could regain her composure and return to the room. The isolation must have been brutal for her because I was often lost in confusion during those days in ICU when she couldn't share her concerns with me. I can't imagine what Rhonda went through, but she never showed me how scared she was. She was incredibly strong, and I clung to that strength each day.

The seriousness of surgery was magnified by the questions regarding whether my heart would respond and begin working again. Each day we waited anxiously to see my level of heart function. Rhonda lived at the hospital. When I was moved to a private room, she slept on a little bench at the end of my bed, keeping constant vigil. The staff brought her a pillow and a blanket to help her be as comfortable as possible. They let her shower in a private room and gave her snacks each day. I'm thankful for the kindness they showed to us.

On my 49th birthday, I was lying in a bed at the Cleveland Clinic instead of playing in a game with my softball team. I felt grateful to be alive yet still in shock this defective valve had been a part of me my whole life and I did not know. It was surreal.

Now it was time to work at getting my strength back. Each day I was required to get out of bed (difficult with extreme pain in my chest, wires, and a drain tube hanging from an IV stand) to walk up and down the hallways. I did this two to three times a day with Rhonda by my side with each step I took. The nurses encouraged me to eat to help get nutrition into my body to promote healing. The problem was that nothing tasted good, not even my favorites. A few bites and I would be full and could not force any more down. It's crazy because I'm such a foodie, but again, nothing tasted good.

I couldn't wait for the day to finally arrive when I would be released from that hospital. There was still the issue of drain tubes that needed to be removed. The doctor needed first to remove some of the stitches keeping my skin surrounding the tubing in my chest. Once the stitches were removed, he asked if I was ready for the tough part. I was. He instructed me to hold onto the hospital bed handrails and said it would be rough. With Rhonda standing at the foot of the bed watching, my doctor pulled and pulled what seemed two to three feet of hoses from my chest. The tubes came flying out with the last hard tug, as did blood and viscous fluids that splattered Rhonda and hit the back wall. My doctor apologized for the mess, never expecting that result to happen. Never a dull moment in my life.

The release day arrived when my doctor walked through my hospital room doorway, stood next to my bed and asked if I was ready to go home. I was so ready! He looked at all the monitors hanging behind me on the wall and hooked to me. He then looked at me with concern and asked me if I was feeling anything in my chest. "Nothing but the wires attached to my skin," I replied. Although I couldn't feel it, I had experienced another setback. I was in Atrial Fibrillation (AFib), a quivering or irregular heartbeat. I was immediately prepared for electrical cardioversion, a process by which the heart is shocked back into a normal rhythm. This extended my stay for another two days and created a new level of concern for my recovery, but thankfully, the cardioversion succeeded. The day of my release from the Cleveland Clinic, my doctor walked into my room, stood by my bed, looked at the monitors and said, "Okay, are you ready to go home now?" We both laughed.

Living in Northeast Ohio gave me access to some of the best cardiovascular surgeons in the country and they saved my life. After 18 days and two hospital stays, they sent me home with strict guidelines of what I could and could not do during recovery and a heart-shaped pillow to squeeze against my chest for the drive home. It helped with the bumpy ride and when I needed to sneeze or cough.

I felt fragile.

In my entire life, I had never felt physically weak. I've been a big guy, an athlete, and the person you call to help you move furniture or work on a home project. My daytime job in quality assurance in the corporate world mainly consisted of using my brain, so I craved physical activity. Now, suddenly I had to carry a pillow the hospital gave me to ride in the car to protect my chest. A sneeze could tear open my incisions. The contrast from being able to do anything I wanted to do to being afraid of doing anything at all, was immense.

Although I couldn't do the things I loved, coming home didn't mean sitting around and doing nothing either. I needed therapy. Cardiac rehabilitation was intense at the beginning, but I slowly recovered. I pushed myself each day because I knew it was needed to regain what I had lost. Life returned to a new type of normal. I learned to eat a low-sodium diet and I exercised every day. I started by walking to my mailbox and back. To my surprise, this short distance was difficult at first. Each day was challenging and frustrating until I could increase the distance. My heart function slowly increased, and after 7 long months, I was released to return to work. I never thought I would miss going to work but I did! My major concern at that point in my recovery was the toll my illness had taken on Rhonda. She is the strongest person I know but everyone has a limit. I was determined to recover my health to have normal lives again and slowly, things improved.

On my 50th birthday, Rhonda threw a surprise party. My

friend Ron had taken me out for a round of golf, hiding the fact Rhonda, Hope, and Jordyn were preparing food, our house, and our yard for this celebration. When we pulled up to my house, I saw many vehicles in my driveway and road. I looked at Ron and he was smiling, and I knew right then what was going on. We walked into the back yard where I was greeted with applause.

Have you ever been applauded by one hundred of your closest family and friends? I have and it's exhilarating! I didn't do anything special; I lived and had a birthday, that's all. I waded through the guests greeting, hugging and thanking each one who came. It was a very hot day, so Rhonda had all the food in the walkout basement, where it was much cooler. The basement was decorated with streamers, balloons and pictures of my baseball accolades hanging on the walls. This party had my favorite theme, baseball! There was a cake decorated in a baseball theme and more food than all of us could possibly eat. Probably the biggest surprise was a giant blowup screen in the yard, where we watched my favorite baseball movie, *The Sandlot*, when it became dark. Watching that movie under the stars and eating popcorn was simply magical.

I was overwhelmed as I reflected on what had happened in one year. I was happy to be alive and celebrating. It's so easy to take life for granted when you're healthy. When I walked into the party, I was greeted by so many friends and family who had been with me over this year of healing. My mind returned to the hospital, the full year of recovery, and what it took to be there on that day. The exhilaration of all those thoughts made the party extremely special. I was happy to be feeling well and celebrating with all these amazing people.

Two years later, as we approached the three-year date post-surgery, my health and my life were looking pretty good. I was doing everything I did before surgery, including working and playing softball. Rhonda and I wanted to celebrate our 30th anniversary in a big way because we realized how different things could have been, and we were grateful for a second act. Our friends, Ron and Hope, suggested a cruise for this grand occasion, and we all went together. I wanted Rhonda to have a stress-free fun vacation because she deserved to relax and not be responsible for anything. Although I had improved, my heart condition had changed our lives significantly, and it was still hard for me to watch the toll it had taken on Rhonda. I wanted to celebrate the gift of our marriage and our future together.

The first night of the cruise, we saw a few shows, danced, and enjoyed the time with each other and our friends. As we stood on the ship's outer balcony with the breeze of ocean air on our faces, we felt renewed. We toasted, believing that the worst was over and now we could cherish life fully. I felt great and looked forward to our snorkeling outing the next day in Freeport, never anticipating what would go so wrong on the beach in Nassau just another day later.

CHAPTER 2

The Crashing Wave

"When Everything Went Quiet..."

W aking up on the second full day of the cruise felt as great as the previous night when we left Freeport. On this morning, our ship docked in the port of Nassau, Bahamas, and we were ready for an adventure. We left the ship and made our way past the many shore excursion companies, hailing a cab to take us to the beach. Upon arriving at our destination, we rented chairs and set up our site with nothing to do but relax and enjoy. The wind was strong, but the beach was still packed with people.

Rhonda and Hope sat together reading as kids ran and played everywhere. Ron and Hope's teenage daughter, Kelsey, and her friend, Heather, walked up and down the shoreline with their feet in the water looking for shells. The sound of waves and the sea breeze filled the air. It was everything I imagined our vacation would be.

I do not like to sit still, so I'm not a big fan of sunbathing. I generally need to be engaged in some type of activity. On that day, it seemed the emerald, blue water kept calling to me, so Ron and I got in and out a few times, swimming out further into the ocean each time, diving through the rolling waves. The water was warm yet refreshing. We had been swimming for a while when I decided I was fatigued and should go back to our chairs for a rest. I began walking through the water toward the shore. When I was in water between knee-high and waist-high, I noticed the sand was different from what I was accustomed to, with a texture more like crushed seashells, unlike normal sand. Every step I took, I sank a little deeper, making it hard to walk. It was such an odd sensation on the bottom of my feet.

And then it happened. I remember looking at the chairs ahead as I lost my footing and a wave came down around my head, engulfing me and planting my face hard in the sand at the bottom of the ocean. I heard a "ca-chunk" sound like crunching steel, reminiscent of the presses in the stamping plant where I used to work. The image of those presses filled my mind as the sound vibrated through my body.

Loud. Intense. Then I felt a sharp pain in my face, and I saw a spectacular explosion of shooting stars and speckles of light dancing around on my eyelids.

And then there was nothing.

There was nothing at all except the swirling water. I could feel my face scraping the ocean floor, and I sensed the water churning like a washing machine around me. The feeling of being pulled backward was strong and odd.

I could not feel my body, but I could still sense the water's motion.

I opened my eyes.

It had been a cloudy day, and I realized the sun must have just come out because I could see beams of light slicing through the water and bouncing off the ocean floor in front of my face. Glorious, brilliant beams of light were shining, and tropical fish swam all around me. Breathtaking. I remember thinking I could not see those fish when I was standing above the water and how amazing they looked from this angle. As I watched them flit around, I became aware of the silence. There was no sound. Everything felt surreal. I was captivated, captivated by the silence, by the beauty of the light beams, and by the fish.

Then I sensed motion.

My mind focused on the feeling of being tugged in and out by another wave.

This new awareness snapped me out of my daze, and I simultaneously realized that I was running out of air. Panic hit. Fear engulfed me. It was bizarre because my mind was whirling, but none of the physical symptoms of panic were happening. My heart wasn't racing. My body didn't feel tense.

I was frozen in the moment as I felt the seconds tick by. I tried to figure out what to do and I wondered why my body was not reacting. I knew every second without action was a second that might cost me my life. I prayed that God wouldn't allow me to drown, but no one came. Then another wave...my face kept scraping off the ocean floor and more churning water.

I kept telling myself to stand up—but I couldn't. My voice screamed in my head. STAND UP! STAND UP! STAND UP!

I wanted to drown—quickly!

My mind flashed back to when I was swimming in our pool with my young son, Brandon. When he was a pre-teen, we were in that pool all summer long. We liked to race underwater, and I usually won because I could hold my breath for so long. I knew I had been under this water much longer than any race with Brandon. I knew how long my lungs could hold out without a breath, and I knew that time was almost over. My capacity to hold my breath was rapidly decreasing. Now I was in a race for my life.

Pull. Tug. Another wave. I hit the ocean floor over and over like a shell tossed by the surf. I was running out of time. My thoughts continued screaming at me. I was nearing the end of what I could endure. My mind was in hyperdrive processing the situation. I knew that if I gasped for breath I would slowly, brutally drown. I decided that it would be best to just suck in as much water as I could, as fast as I could, so I would drown quickly. It became clear. I knew what I had to do. I never thought there would come a time in my life I would realize the precise moment my life was about to end. But that very moment was here.

My internal dialogue grew louder, yelling the words, "I'm almost out of air! I'm almost out! Are you going to do it?"

All I could think about was that I needed to take control of my last moments of life and not let this be an agonizing death filled with suffering. I knew I needed to execute my plan. The words swirled with the water. I'm almost out of air. I'm almost out of air. You have to do it, John. Be brave. Just take a deep breath....

And then I saw the top of the water. Feet. Legs. A breath of air filling my lungs as my screaming mind quieted, and I could hear a voice. It was Ron asking me if I was okay.

When Ron saw me from afar, he was about ten yards away. I was floating face down in the water; he thought I had a heart attack. He yelled for help as he and three young men moved quickly to get me out of the surf. Ron asked me what was wrong and somehow, I responded, "This isn't good." He realized right away that it wasn't my heart when he saw I wasn't able to help myself get out of the water.

Just a few more seconds and it would have been too late. Ron and those young men saved my life.

It was the oddest sensation seeing the top of the water and not immediately understanding how I was hovering above it. I could not feel the four men holding my arms and legs. I was overwhelmed by the sounds and by the brightness of the sun reflecting off the waves. I could breathe, but I had no sensory perception of what was happening. I knew I was taking in the air with each breath, but I could not feel my body. I could not see what had happened physically. All I could see were feet and legs.

The feelings I had just experienced under the water were intensified when I was back on the shore and started breathing. I was overwhelmed with emotions. Fear. Panic. Gratitude. Confusion. Pain. Wonder. Peace. Resolve. Terror. All of it.

The next thing I felt were hands on my head and voices saying, "Stabilize him...flip him over, slowly."

And then I saw the faces around me. People were crying. A crowd had formed, and when I saw Rhonda and Hope, I felt their fear. I felt hands on my head and my face. I watched as someone flipped me around and I saw limbs of my body, but I did not understand why those flipping limbs weren't registering pain or any other sensation.

I felt strange. My mind was stunned. The adrenaline rush that kept me alive under that water had also made me acutely aware of my surroundings. It was like when you get into a quiet car and start the engine, then to be shocked by a blasting radio that your teenage son left on when he drove the car last. The noise around me felt like that loud blast of noise, but I could not turn it down, so it just got more intense. The light was blinding, the sounds were overwhelming, and I could not connect the facts. I knew that I could not feel my body. I knew people were upset. I knew the situation was bad. I just didn't know how grim it was.

During all this commotion, I looked at all those people touching my body, and I realized I could not feel their hands. I felt nothing. At that moment, the words emerged in my mind, "I am paralyzed."

Amid the confusion and chatter from the crowd surrounding me, I saw Rhonda and somehow heard her say, "I love you." The next voice I heard came from a man who was kneeling close to me. That same voice had said, "...flip him over, slowly." With both hands on my head, holding it straight, he told me he was a doctor—I discovered later that he was from Israel. He said he knew the island well, and he had precise instructions for what needed to happen next regarding my care. I later learned that his quick actions not only kept me alive, but they kept me alive with the possibility of recovery.

Lying on the shore, all I could see were the anguished faces of the people surrounding me. I felt their fear. Intense hopelessness overcame me. Physical dread.

In the water, I kept saying to myself, "Stand up. What are you doing? STAND UP!" but I didn't fully understand the gravity of what had happened. As I read the people's faces, their expressions told me how serious it was. I felt their hopelessness. Their horror at seeing my injury added to my horror. Desperation grew, creeping into every thought, every corner of my mind.

CHAPTER 3

Darkness From The Depths
— A Familiar Desperation

"How do we go on?"

I grew up in Port Huron, 60 miles northeast of Detroit, Michigan, along the St. Clair River. The St. Clair River, forty and a half miles long, drains Lake Huron into Lake St. Clair. It's a significant component in the Great Lakes Waterway, with shipping channels permitting cargo vessels to travel between the upper and lower Great Lakes. When we were young, the river was a sanctuary for me and my friends. Large freighters carrying cargo to many destinations would glide through the river's strong current, mesmerizing me as I sat on the shoreline. It was unbelievably blue in the sunshine, as turquoise as the Caribbean Ocean and served as a place to fish, swim, and cool off in the hot summer months, which we often did.

My neighborhood had well-groomed yards maintained by hard-working blue-collar families. Children always seemed to be playing on the sidewalks, on the streets, and in the yards, making friends was easy.

These were simpler times in my life when every day was an adventure, and my quest was to be outside playing no matter the season or the weather. These are the joyful memories that stay fresh in my mind and help balance out the dark clouds that hovered over much of my childhood.

The first time I remember feeling the darkness was when I was thirteen years old. Like most boys my age, I had a close group of friends in my neighborhood, and we spent many of our days hanging out together, finding something to entertain ourselves. One of our favorite things was riding our bikes around our hometown. It was harmless fun and a good way to enjoy the freedom of being a kid.

Growing up in Michigan meant that winters were long, and spring, summer and fall were for playing hard anytime you had the chance. On one of those unusually warm autumn days, my next-door neighbor, Alvin, came over to see what I was doing. I will never forget him. He was a skinny little kid, a few years younger than me, with skin as white as snow. Because he was one of the neighborhood's younger kids, he was excited when he got to hang out with us. I know it was very cool for me when the older guys would allow me to play baseball with them when they needed an extra player, and I think he felt the same way.

That day Alvin and I set off and met up with a few other

friends. The weather was perfect, warm and sunny, so we decided as a group to ride our bikes into the city. Back then, the city was filled with retail stores and a lot of people who frequented them. This day was no different. We wove in and around the crowds so much that I'm shocked we never ran into any people.

I can still hear the laughter of my friends and feel the thrill of riding that day. We eventually rode away from the downtown area as we headed back home towards our neighborhood. I remember flying down the hill with the rest of the guys and past the fire station situated along the Black River, feeling the freedom that comes with speed. Alvin was usually at the back of the pack. His bike was old and rickety, but he was a tough little kid and usually did well keeping up with us.

Most days, when we were tired of riding our bikes, we would play red rover, capture the flag, or baseball. It never took long to decide on another activity. We always added or subtracted friends depending on who got called for lunch or dinner or who got summoned in to do chores. Faces changed throughout the day, and we didn't care as long as we had enough kids to play. This day was no different.

Our games concluded as the daylight faded. Many of my friends had the same strict curfew as I did, "Be home before the streetlights come on."

About fifteen minutes after I arrived home, there was a knock at the door. It was Alvin's mother, wondering if he was with me. He was not. I remember that she left and then quickly returned, telling us he had not come home. I recall the sick feeling in my stomach since this was not like him—not to be home when he should be.

Minutes passed. As news traveled from home to home, people from the neighborhood searched for Alvin. These were the days when most families in the neighborhood knew one another and rarely locked their doors. His name echoed throughout the streets. Panic set in.

Eventually, the police arrived at Alvin's home, with many neighbors and my friends still standing there. The two officers exited their police cruiser and entered the house and reappeared a short while later. The officers questioned us, asking me and my friends when we last saw Alvin. We had to piece together when we thought that last time was. We had the bike ride, played a few games in a neighbor's yard, dinner, then more games in the neighborhood before the streetlights came on. Oddly, I didn't remember seeing him since our bike ride. Somehow, no one seemed to remember seeing him after passing the fire station on our bike ride.

Hours turned to days. Fear built.

I felt frozen with fear of what had happened to my friend and had difficulty sleeping. My friends and I were so scared as our minds swirled with questions. Did someone kidnap him? Did he get lost? Where could he be?

A few days later, the news nobody wanted to hear arrived. Divers found Alvin's body in the murky, dark Black River near the fire station. The police told Alvin's family that their investigation revealed that he probably lost control riding down the hill because of his high rate of speed and lack of brakes. He and his bike sped down the hill and flew directly into the river.

None of us had heard a sound. Not a cry. Not a shout.

Alvin had gone under that water and drowned alone.

At the funeral, I was numb. We were just a bunch of boys riding our bikes and having fun and then suddenly, Alvin was gone.

It didn't make sense to my thirteen-year-old brain. How could we live knowing he was dead?

How could we go on like everything was normal? The sadness was overwhelming. It felt like a piece of us was missing, and it took a while before my friends and I stopped talking about it every time we saw each other. Nothing felt the same. When we tried to play our typical games, it didn't feel right. It didn't matter how nice the weather was or what we were eating, nothing felt right. Tragedy has a way of changing everything, and sometime that year it happened to us—we accepted our new normal. We had learned that death can come instantly, and we could no longer be the carefree kids we had once been.

CHAPTER 4
Everything Changes

The Changing Tide

A few years earlier, in 1971, my life at home began to unravel. My dad, who was the center of my world, moved out. I was unaware of why he left. I thought he didn't want to be with our family anymore and had deserted us. I idolized my dad, and I was devastated. My dad had a love and passion for baseball that seemed to equal mine. We talked about the subject quite often, which seemed to fuel my constant thoughts and desire to play this game I loved. I would sit at his softball games, amazed by his skill, and dream of the day I could play on the same team as him. He was my stability, and his departure made me wake up to the fact that our family was not what I had thought. My image of a safe home crumbled.

My parents had met in Germany when my dad, who was enlisted in the Army, was stationed at Monteith Barracks, an Army installation in my mother's hometown of Furth. He was in the 4th Armored Division, Tank Gunnery. My father graduated high school in the summer of 1956 and joined the Army by September of the same year. His records and medals show he had an impressive nine-year career until his retirement in 1965.

My mother already had a two-year-old daughter when she met my father, and he adopted her when she was about five years old. I was born in Germany in June of 1961, fourteen days before my parents married. I was three years old when the army moved our family to Fort Riley, Kansas, where my two younger sisters, Maryann and Diane, were born and where we stayed until my father's honorable discharge. He had fulfilled his enlistment terms, and that meant we were moving again. Kansas was not the place we would call home.

One of my earliest memories is turning five in our house in Port Huron, Michigan. Interestingly, it was the home my dad grew up in, which he had bought from his mother, my grandmother. The house was old and needed a lot of updating. The kitchen cabinets were falling apart, so when a friend of the family offered cabinets from their home that suffered a fire, my parents jumped on the offer.

There were four of us children to share two bedrooms, so my parent's friends helped build wooden bunk beds in both rooms. Old carpeting was ripped out and replaced and wooden paneling attached to the walls. The small bathroom needed a complete redo, including toilet, bathtub, sink and plumbing. The house needed work. Our family didn't care because it was much better than the government housing we had previously lived in, and more important, it was our home! In Kansas, we lived with so many other families in close quarters, and it did not allow for much privacy or space to roam.

We were all happy for a change in our living situation, and my Dad was happy to move back to his hometown, taking a third shift position for a company in the automotive industry. For a few years, life was good, and it gave us a sense of security.

Our mom was comfortable and settled as a stay-at-home mother. In those years, Mom always seemed happy and full of life. I have fond memories of days when she would play board games and cards or make homemade hard candy on the stove with us children. She loved gardening and took pride in all the beautiful flowers she cultivated. Neighbors would occasionally stop and comment about our yard, doling out compliments about the time and care my mother took with her plants. Even as a child, I was impressed to watch her work hard to transform our yard into stunning flower displays.

It's hard to grasp how much life changed from those early days in Port Huron. I have no memory of my parents arguing in front of us children. I do, however, clearly remember the day an emergency vehicle pulled up to the house with sirens blaring. My mother met them at the front door, yelling at us kids to get out of their way. She led the emergency responders to my parent's bedroom. There was so much commotion, and I had no understanding of what was happening. Standing in our living room when they emerged, I saw my father on a stretcher with his eyes closed and an oxygen mask on his face. There was no talking, only shock and confusion for me and my siblings. My mother was weeping. I recall asking my mother what happened as they pulled away with my father secured in the ambulance. What was going on? She replied that my dad was sick and needed to be in the hospital. He was gone for what seemed to be weeks, and when he returned home, we never knew what had happened. Life went back to normal.

It was not until later in life I learned my father had attempted suicide by ingesting an entire bottle of sleeping pills because he was devastated that my mother had asked him for a divorce. When they transported him to our local hospital, he was intubated, and his stomach was pumped to remove all the toxins. They saved his life, but the problems that led to his overdose were not addressed. This was never discussed with us children, and about a year later, without warning, my dad suddenly left us. I remember him carrying out trash bags of clothes and shoes to his car, our family's car, without a word spoken. I saw him drive away.

You would think that my mom would have been happy since she had asked for a divorce, but that is not what happened. After my dad left our home, my mother struggled with anger. Her outbursts were frightening. She would go on tirades for hours, crying, and using guilt to control us. She would tell us how lucky we were by constantly comparing our "spoiled" life to her childhood in Germany, a country devastated by war. Her rampages were sparked by the smallest of things. Shoes left at the door were as upsetting as an "F" on our report card. There was no way to gauge what would set her off. At her worst, she would beat us with whatever she could grab. A wooden spoon, a switch, a shoe, a hanger, and even a dead goose! My oldest sister became the target and was hit by the dead goose after some remark she had made to my mother. These things all served as weapons to punish us.

When she was especially angry with me, she would lock me in our cellar, shutting off the lights, and leave me there for what seemed like hours. The cellar was practically a dungeon. Our basement was what's known as a Michigan basement. They start as a crawl space, only to be later excavated to the depth of a basement but mostly shallower, as was ours. Our side walls had exposed dirt extending in two feet that was later covered with wood. The cellar could only be accessed through a trapdoor in the floor of a spare bedroom and had no windows, making it dark, damp, musty and infested with mice.

We had an old closet, constructed of slatted wood used specifically to store our canning jars. It was filled with beans, tomatoes, beets, apple sauce or anything else my mother canned. Every time you opened the door to that closet, the mice scattered. The times I spent sitting at the bottom of the stairs waiting to be let upstairs again, I would hear the mice scratching. My older sister remembers being locked down there too, so it must not have been just my special punishment.

I had desperate moments in that cellar, never knowing how long she would keep me there. The absolute darkness does something to a child's mind so confusing it just shuts you down. When she would force me into the cellar, I would close my eyes and lean up against the wall and try really hard not to think about where I was. It was so isolating and scary, but I told no one about it. Not my friends. Not my dad. I never felt the desire to share it because I could not understand why my mom would do such a bizarre thing to me. Strangely, through it all, I always knew that my mother loved me and that she would turn back to her nice self eventually. I was a pretty optimistic and happy person despite all the chaos. Surely these things happened to other people, right? I always wanted to help my mom to feel happy, however, I did not know how I could change things for her. I did not understand bipolar depression then, but I witnessed some of its effects when it reared its ugly head in my house.

When my dad left, my mother took the role of the sole disciplinarian seriously. My dad was strict, but his discipline made sense. If we did something wrong, we were punished. He could get angry but it was only if we had pushed his patience and not listened to him. We could gauge his reactions, unlike our unpredictable mother. I think she learned her tactics from her mother, who also was a single parent in Germany. My mother often told us how much she hated her mother for the things she did to her, yet my mom did the same things. It was ironic to hear her complaints about her life while watching her recreate the same dynamic in our home.

Oddly enough, in 1971, shortly after my parents separated, they took the four of us to Disney World in Florida. My parents were still separated, but my father, who lived with my aunt and uncle in our city, had visitation with us bi-weekly. It was the first year the park was open, and we were so excited. We were very poor and rarely got to experience things like vacations. Disney World was beyond our comprehension. It was an extremely long trip with all six of us crammed in a car anticipating the fun we would have together. Going to Disney World with both of our parents seemed like a dream come true. It was coupled with getting to stay at a relative's home in Florida, which was a surprise to all of us kids. We saw and experienced many new things like palm trees, swimming in the ocean, and eating at restaurants. Driving from Michigan to Florida was a hopeful time, yet it was still very confusing. I could not understand why my parents, who were separated for the last six months, were acting and functioning like we were an intact family. I really thought everything would be fine, and maybe this would bring them back together permanently.

I could not have been more wrong. We returned home, and my dad left again. It was over. How could this happen? Why did this happen? I am not sure if he thought there was a chance to reconcile because we never talked about it. The vacation was magical, everything seemed fine, but it was just on the surface. Dad was gone, and there was nothing I could do about it. It was official, December 1972, my parent's divorce was final. The divorce crushed the hope I had held onto that we would have dad back, and our lives would be better, and now I had to let it go.

After the Disney trip, my dad moved on and started dating a woman named Donna. By October of 1973, he married her and moved into a mobile home with her and her four children at the northern end of our city. Donna was great and treated us like her own, helping to make a difficult situation a little bit easier. We were just like the Brady Bunch (TV show from the 70s), a big, blended family, so I felt like things were going to be okay for all of us. We had adjustments to make to combine this new group, as you can imagine. Donna's children, Doug, Cindy, David, and Cherie became family to us. It was awkward initially, but we learned to be comfortable with each other in a short period. My three sisters and I went for regular weekend visits, each time finding out something new about our new siblings.

We learned each other's likes and dislikes the more time we stayed with them. David and I were the same age, so getting to know him was easy. He would allow me to hang out with him and his friends from the neighborhood, playing baseball and riding dirt bikes. Doug was the oldest. I remember he had a beautiful Camaro and loved turning the music up really loud as he drove us back and forth to church. I really looked up to him. Cindy and Cherie were so loving, kind, and fun, and they both had infectious laughs. We would often sit down with a bowl of popcorn, watch movies, tell funny stories, and laugh for hours. It was great being able to laugh again in a family setting. This union of new siblings and stepmother gave me a renewed excitement of belonging. This was something I had been missing in my life. Even today, I really miss those moments.

When my father departed from my everyday life, my world had crumbled, creating a sense of deep loss. Being with my blended family helped me to heal some of that loss, and I started putting some of those broken pieces back together. Mom was in a continual cycle of good and bad, but often being at my dad's place gave me a greater sense of stability.

My sisters and I developed a routine of going for our weekend visits, and on the surface, everything was good until one night when it went bad quickly. On this night, my dad and Donna had a group of friends over, and they were all drinking and playing cards at the kitchen table. Through their laughter, I could hear my dad saying terrible things about my mom. He said, "I am glad I'm not with that *expletive* (my mother's name) anymore." He had many horrible things to say about my mother, followed by even more expletives! He went on and on until I finally went into the kitchen and asked him to stop.

My anger was stronger than my fear of my dad. Even at twelve years of age, I knew it was wrong for him to talk like that about my mom, and I had the strong urge to defend her. He was instantly furious with me for speaking to him about his behavior. Screaming at me in a rage, he told me he would talk about whatever he wanted to talk about in his own home. I asked him again to stop, and he told me if I did not like it, he would take me home. I told him to take my sisters and me home. He told me we could never come back if we left. I felt we had no choice but to leave. I was backed into a corner, and if I stayed, I would betray my mom. We all would.

He took us home.

After that day, there were no more visitation weekends. My dad never showed up at my baseball games. He never called.

I remember my sisters MaryAnn and Diane crying in the car on that trip back home because our dad said we would not get our Christmas presents that year or any other year, even though Christmas was just a few weeks away. He said he was taking them all back to the store. You could see his anger through his raised eyebrows and red face as he barked out his threats of no presents.

My dad normally had a calm demeanor and a smile. This was scary. His face was bright red, and I felt the heat radiating from his anger could have melted the snow that was falling. He was so enraged! My dad drove a large, long station wagon, and I felt like crawling into the very back seat, but I stayed in the front passenger seat and felt his emotions pelting me. Even though it was only 20 minutes long, that car ride felt like it would never end.

It was jarring to be in the middle of an extended stepfamily with lots of interaction one minute and then to be told we would have no contact with any of them at all. We loved each other, and now they would be taken away at a very vulnerable time in our lives. It did not seem like it could really be happening, but I could feel his intensity increasing, and my hope for resolution sank in direct proportion.

We were dropped off at home to face our mother's fury. I told her the things my dad had said around the table that night. I knew then that it must have been difficult for her to hear, yet I knew I had to tell her the truth even though it hurt her. Life felt confusing and desperate. There was no way to do the right thing for everyone that night. I stood up for my mom and subsequently lost my dad. If I had said nothing, I would have kept my dad but lost respect for myself for betraying my mom. My nature is to try to help people. This was a difficult time for me because my decision was not all about me. That decision also affected my sisters and stepfamily. My sisters and I stayed close to each other and tried to stay strong. It was clear that our lives as we knew them had changed forever.

Around this same time, my mom began to go away, and my siblings and I would have to stay with other people. She never told us where she was going, but she always left after one of her bad episodes. These times were filled with screaming, crying fits, and sleeping for days, only emerging to rage or use the bathroom. Eventually, many years later, I realized that she was admitted to a psychiatric floor at a local hospital for her nervous breakdowns. I did not understand this until I was much older. My only understanding in those times when my mother would be depressed or screaming at us was that when the episodes happened, she would go away for a while. When she left, the length of time was never the same. At times she was gone for a few weeks, and other times she was gone longer. It was always an upsetting experience.

The worst episodes were when we were left with people we did not know. We were young children who were told very little except we would be staying with strangers for a while. It was completely disruptive. My sisters and I were often separated from each other and had to stay with different people. To this day, I am not sure if we were placed in someone's home by Child Protective Services or if people just took us who knew our family issues. Communication was sparse, and our lives stayed in a basic state of chaos.

Through all her hospitalizations, to my knowledge, my dad never checked on us. We were alone in the world. Then suddenly, Mom would come back, and we would get into a routine again until the next episode. How could this be happening? Why wasn't Dad helping?

My escape was baseball. I loved playing it. I loved watching it. I was consumed with baseball. Don't get me wrong, I loved baseball before all this turmoil, but it became my avenue of escape when life was difficult. Life for me became living and breathing baseball. It didn't matter if it was a pickup game, a game of pickle, Whiffle ball, or hitting pop-ups in the street; if it was baseball, I was playing it. If I had no one to play with, I would take a rubber ball and my glove and walk to our local school. I would throw the ball at the school building's brick wall so that it would bounce back to me, literally playing catch with the wall. I didn't have to do that often because my friends and I played baseball almost every day. I seriously played baseball every day if it didn't rain too hard. In spring, summer, and fall, the rain was my nemesis. If my games were canceled because of it, I would stand in the window and cry, watching it fall from the sky as if my tears would somehow make it stop. Yeah, I would say playing baseball was all I wanted to do.

My little league games were miles away from my house, so I had to ride my bike a long way to get to the ballpark. I always hoped to look up in the stands and see my dad. One day he finally did show up to a game, but it was because my stepbrother, David, was playing on the other team. David and I were the same age, and our teams were in the playoffs, facing each other.

I will never forget the heartache of watching my dad cheer for David when he came to the plate. He never even looked at me whenever I glanced his way. I cannot explain the deep scar that day left on my heart. I was unfamiliar with divorce until it happened to my family. I had never heard anyone talk about divorce. It was not a familiar concept. I learned quickly, at a very young age, the kind of pain it can create. As I was experiencing all these horrible emotions for the first time and trying to deal with them, my mind fixated on the idea that if I ever were to marry, I didn't want my future family to feel this pain. It became a strong, driving force for me never to feel this way again and to not let other people feel this way either.

Life went on. I grew older and learned to survive the bad times. I had good friends and stayed busy with sports and eventually work. I tried not to dwell on the anger and the hurt and attempted not to think about how much I missed having my dad in my life. My sisters and I were getting more independent and finding our own paths.

When I was between seventeen and eighteen years old, I walked into the house after work and heard my mom and my older sister discussing my dad. They were not aware I was standing there listening when I heard the unthinkable. They were talking about how he had sexually abused my sister!

WHAT?

I heard my mom say, "It has been so hard on me since I made him leave, even after his suicide attempt." My sister reacted much the same but replied, "You have no idea how hard it has been on me!" A small argument ensued as to who had struggled the most through this horrific period in time. I couldn't stand there any longer and I entered the room. I was too young to confront what I had overheard and acted as if I had just arrived home. That conversation ended abruptly. I never let on that I had overheard, and I have carried this secret from both until this writing.

I was devastated.

Who was this man I had admired so much? Who was this man who had abandoned us? Who was this man who had wounded my mom and shattered my sister? I was confused and angry. I had so many questions, and at the same time, the details of my life were making more sense. As the information sunk in, I could see how his choices had caused us all to lose so much. It was like watching pieces falling into place in a previously unsolvable puzzle.

My heart ached for my sister. This was a disturbing secret she kept locked away deep inside, hiding it from the world. I could not imagine the hurt and the confusion amid so many other emotions she must have felt. The thought she had been expected to go there to visit on weekends after this happened was also horrifying. It made no sense to divorce my dad to protect my sister and then send her to his house with no protection. Even her siblings did not know and therefore could not help her.

I had lingering questions. Why did my mom not tell us why she divorced him? It was too much to process. So many nights, I had wondered if we had done something wrong to make him leave. Had we known about the abuse, it would have helped us all to understand what my mom and sister were going through so we could support them. However, I cannot begin to understand the trauma that either one of them experienced. This was a time when sexual abuse was not discussed in "proper society."

I wanted to ask my dad what had happened, but he was out

of my life. Remembering the night he took us home and vowed never to see us again gave me a new perspective on his behavior. At that moment, a deep hatred grew in my heart toward him. I could not escape it.

CHAPTER 5
Low Tide

Another Loss

My dad's anger was like a slow boil right below my level of consciousness that I had no way to express. It stayed buried deep inside like lava in a quietly simmering volcano, but it was always there beneath the surface. Most of the time, I could stay distracted because I was involved in my own life. I kept busy delivering pizzas for a local pizzeria, playing baseball or any other sport available, and living each day to the fullest like only an eighteen-year-old can do. I had enlisted in the United States Marine Corps and planned to leave after graduation. Life on the surface was going pretty well for me until another event changed the direction of my journey.

In the fall of my senior year of high school, I was riding in my friend's vehicle's back seat when we were involved in an accident. When the vehicle lunged forward, his seat came unhinged, and the weight of both him and his seat came crashing down on me, severely injuring my ankle. I was transported to the hospital, where it was determined that my ankle was shattered. The orthopedic doctor strongly recommended that I not enter the Marine Corps because of the damage. I was pretty upset at the time, but in hindsight, I realize that I stayed in our town because of the accident. After the accident I met Rhonda. Life has a funny way of bringing people together!

I met Rhonda my senior year through her brother, Greg, one of my closest friends. I knew quickly after meeting her she was special. I loved spending time with her and just getting to know her. When we were together, I felt optimistic about the future. It quickly became apparent that Rhonda was the perfect partner for me. Her positive attitude and beautiful smile would light up a room; these were virtues I really admired. I enjoyed spending time with her family, which was also a bonus for me. I began to envision a way to build my own life and move in a much better direction away from my childhood difficulties. Rhonda's family began to feel like my family, especially Greg since we were already friends. The emotional "lava" was controlled when my mind was occupied with good, positive things.

Our city was fairly large, with over thirty thousand people, so it was easy to find good things to stay occupied. Greg and I knew each other from high school and shared interests like driving fast cars, cruising our city's long main drag through town, listening to music, and sharing good times with friends. Greg loved to have fun and had an infectious smile. He always had some funny story or comment that made people laugh. I guess it was one of his qualities that attracted me to forge a strong friendship. Laughter bonded us as friends. Neither of us wanted to take things too seriously.

I will never forget the warm Saturday afternoon that Greg and I were hanging out at his house eating a sandwich before I had to go to work. Saturday was our busiest delivery night, but Greg wanted me to call off work and go to a party with him and two of our other friends. I wanted to go but felt bad calling off. His light-hearted banter finally convinced me to call in sick, so I phoned from his house. The manager believed my fabricated story about being sick and told me he hoped I would feel better and would see me tomorrow. I thought I was off the hook. We stayed at his house until it was time to leave to pick up our other friends. As we walked out the front door, the phone rang, and Greg went back in to answer it. It was my sister Diane, so he handed me the phone. She told me that my manager at work had called the house, claiming there was an emergency. I didn't want to call him back because of lying to him.

I struggled with my conscience but finally called. He told me that the other delivery driver had been in a car accident and couldn't come to work because his car was completely disabled. The pizzeria manager was desperate because there were only two drivers, and he was hoping I wasn't too sick to drive. Assuring him I would be okay and would be there for the shift, Greg and I separated with a plan to reconnect at the end of the night. He left to go pick up our friends who were going to the party as I went to work. We agreed to meet up at 1 am in the center of town when I finished my shift, hoping to salvage my evening. We often hung out that late, so it should have been a typical evening for us. Work was busy as usual, which helped me to let go of the idea that I was missing the party, but I was looking forward to hearing about it from Greg later.

It was a little before 1 am when I arrived at our designated meeting spot with a six-pack of beer and a warm pizza and waited for Greg. At around 2:00 am, I gave up and went home, wondering what had happened. Greg was a reliable guy, so something seemed off. I didn't want to call his house and wake anyone up if he just forgot. I went to bed and figured I would find out the next day.

In the early morning our house phone rang. It was Rhonda. Greg had been in a horrible accident and was in the hospital. She was sobbing so hard that I could barely understand her. She told me he had been taken by life flight to Detroit, an hour's drive from home. Rhonda told me she and her family were leaving shortly after our conversation ended.

The revelation of Greg's accident, coupled with just waking up so early, caused me to pause. I needed to make sense of what I should do. I showered and dressed, jumped in my car, and drove as fast as I could to get there, racing through the crazy Detroit rush hour traffic, trying to avoid an accident myself. It was a complete blur. I arrived at the hospital and hurried to the front desk, asking where I could find my friend and his family. I was escorted by a nurse who said she would show me where to find them. As we walked into the Intensive Care Unit toward Rhonda and her family, I could see the pain and anguish on each of their faces. I was told of Greg's dire situation; how he was being kept alive on a life support ventilator but without hope of recovery. I wanted to see my friend and asked Rhonda's parents if they would allow me in the room. Rhonda's father extended his hands, touching both of my shoulders. He prepared me for what I was about to see in the next room. He said, "John, I want you to remember Greg the way you last saw him, not the way you will see him now." He told the nursing staff I was family, and he walked me into the room.

Greg was unrecognizable. I remember thinking, this was not my friend laying in the hospital bed. He had a tube down his throat from a ventilator keeping his body breathing. The shock of seeing him left me speechless. My heart was broken not only for me but also for his family. Hours before, I had been waiting to hang out and hear about the party. Hours before, I figured he had just gone home early. A day earlier, our biggest concern was whether I could get out of work so I could go to the party.

I discovered later that while I was driving to work, a drunk driver had gone left of center and hit Greg's car head-on minutes after he picked up another friend and his girlfriend on the way to the party. If Greg hadn't heard the phone ring earlier that night, I would have been in his car. My sister caught me just in time.

Greg and our two friends that were in his car died. The other driver lived, but one of her passengers perished in that horrible crash. It was not her first drunk driving accident. She had killed a child in a previous automobile accident while being highly intoxicated. The laws regarding drinking and driving were weak back then, and the driver only received a sentence of one year in the county jail with daily work release privileges for killing four people. Justice was nonexistent.

We all had to face the loss of our friends and family in a senseless and horrific car accident that should not have happened. I wanted to be supportive of Rhonda's family, so when the case went to trial, I made sure to attend. It was my first time to be part of a court proceeding. As we sat listening to witness after witness giving their testimony, I could not imagine what Rhonda and her family were experiencing. It was so hard for me to hear all the graphic details. I could not imagine the pain they were experiencing in losing a son and a brother. A passenger's testimony in the woman's car showed that she was clearly drunk, and all she received was one year in jail with work release followed by probation. Are you kidding me? We were all in disbelief, and the anger was a physical tension I could not release.

Reflection has a way of humbling me. I realize I had no right to judge since I would drink and drive back then as well. I am so fortunate that my mistakes didn't have the same outcome, but at that moment, there was no rational thought, just anger.

Rhonda's entire family was in shock. It was a horrible time.

The other people in the car who died were also our friends. Our entire community was in a state of mourning.

How do you go on? Such tragic, senseless deaths and I had no way to make sense of the losses or process grief. My mind went numb because the emotions were too intense to experience, leading me to a period of feeling that life was meaningless. The emotional despair cut off all my other emotions. I could not be happy because that felt wrong. How could I enjoy life? Guilt hung over me like a cloud. It was soul-sucking. I remember not wanting to live because I could not see beyond the guilt. I believed that I didn't deserve to be happy because they could not be happy, and that feeling of guilt made me bitter. I felt very little except for anger. I didn't want to be an angry person, so I tried not to feel at all. Numb was much more acceptable than anger. I now understand that anger is often a shield that protects us when we are in shock. It is how we survive. My younger self did not have all the information I do now about trauma and defense mechanisms.

It may seem strange to tie these events together, but the way my emotions were frozen in that time feels similar to the feelings around my accident. It was déjà vu when the words paralyzed landed in my brain, and I began to understand what had happened to my body when the wave hit me, and I hit the ocean floor. I was numb, in shock emotionally and physically, not understanding the gravity but witnessing the horrified reactions of the people around me. I felt like I did that day 33 years before when I saw Greg in that hospital room, understanding it but not understanding it at the level that would eventually come. The emotions were too intense. Numbness hit like the wave.

I know now that shock helps us to survive. At that moment, I knew my situation was very alarming, yet I was somewhat protected so I could not feel the full range of my emotions. Feeling it all at that moment would have overwhelmed me. Shock helps us survive until we can feel, grieve, and start again.

CHAPTER 6
Life or Death

Feeling Lost and Alone

"You smile but you want to cry. You talk but you want to be quiet. You pretend like you're happy, but you are not."

– Unknown

S o, there I was, lying on the beach, asking people to shift so their bodies would block the sunlight blinding me. The beach filled with laughter, the screams from children playing, and the crashing of the waves seemed to go silent for a moment. Many people standing around me whispered as the sound of the ocean rang back into my ears. I lay there so confused. I couldn't see the rest of my body, and I had no idea what had happened to it. I couldn't feel it. All I could see was fear in the eyes looking down at me.

At some point, I realized that although emergency services had been called, no one was coming. Later, I was told that it took thirty minutes or more for the ambulance to arrive at the beach even though the hospital was only a ten-minute drive away. We were experiencing a medical emergency in a different country and we expected that our care would be similar to what we knew. I had never thought about having an emergency outside of the United States and so I assumed that medical care was similar, but the next 36 hours taught me how terrifyingly different it can be.

When the ambulance finally arrived, the doctor from Israel holding my head shouted orders to the Emergency Medical Service crew, telling them I had a critical neck injury and that I needed to be stabilized. I watched them lift me onto a stretcher while at the same time, I could feel nothing except hands on my head and face. The paramedics placed a brace on my neck, extending from my chest to my chin. I could feel the brace touching my chin and it helped during the trip as we drove over bumpy roads that jarred me. It was an odd sensation to feel my head moving alone in space.

The next moments were strange and agonizing. When they pushed my stretcher into the emergency room entrance, no one ran over to me to begin the process of triage. Medically, this was a serious situation, yet there was no commotion. No excitement or urgency like I was expecting. There was no real waiting room like most hospitals I have experienced. From my view, I saw a line of mismatched, decrepit chairs, no front desk, staff just milling around not attending to any patient's needs.

I was given an IV with antibiotics and then nothing

happened. Rhonda maintained an expression of pure terror — tears streaming from her eyes — yet no one even glanced up at her. Eventually, a woman approached us to ask about our insurance, which she claimed was not valid in the Bahamas. She told us that before the hospital would do anything more for me, they would need $10,000.

The world stopped. How would we get $10,000? We had disembarked for an afternoon of beach time with just a wallet, our credit card, and a bit of cash, expecting to be back on board for dinner as we sailed to the next port. Everything was on the ship, including our documents.

Miraculously, our friends had immediately jumped into action as the ambulance drove away with me, but we did not know this at the time. I am still amazed that while we were on our way to the hospital, Ron and Hope had the extraordinary calm and presence of mind to grab a taxi to go back to the ship and retrieve Rhonda's purse and our passports. They grabbed another taxi and brought these items to us before our cruise ship left port. Miraculously, this turned out to be our only way out of the country and out of danger.

The contrast from the accident scene to the hospital bewildered me. On the beach, I had a doctor barking orders at people that I was in critical condition and needed immediate stabilization, but at the hospital, this emotionless woman said they wouldn't touch me unless we secured $10,000.

I believe she would have let me die in the hallway without a second thought.

Although I couldn't turn my head, I could see Rhonda standing there in her beach clothes and a hooded sweatshirt that Hope took off her back. We talked about the money situation, and I could feel all hope drain from her voice. In that moment, Rhonda told me she had no way to get money and no way to help me. In desperation, she tried to explain to the woman she would have to get money wired because we had no money with us. Unmoved by my bleeding facial wounds and paralysis, the woman would not allow any further treatment without cash.

Keeping herself calm and together, Rhonda quickly began making phone calls to her parents and our credit card company to get cash. In the middle of the calls, our cell phone company notified her we did not have an international plan, so she had to call them to pay for a plan. Our provider guaranteed that it would be retroactive, but that never materialized. Later we ended up with an astronomical bill that just added to the mounting financial crisis.

This was more chaos added while Rhonda was trying to get money so I would have care. I still don't know how Rhonda stayed level when things were so out of our control. We had no idea what the expense would be for the life flight to get me back to the United States or what other costs the hospital could throw at us. As she tried to figure things out, all I could do was lay motionless on a gurney in the hallway with people walking casually by, going about their business.

Rhonda's parents wired us money and she eventually convinced our credit card company to increase our line of credit to pay the hospital. After many hours of waiting, our bill for services was paid and I was taken in for X-rays and an MRI. Soon after all the evaluations, a doctor did come in to see me. While I was being examined, Rhonda frantically worked to get an immediate life flight out of Nassau to get to the Cleveland Clinic. The emergency room doctors assessed my injury and realized this was a dire situation and I would need a specialist.

Many hours passed before the specialist, a neuro-surgeon came and spoke with Rhonda. For a while, he had been with me, assessing my injuries, and he finally brought Rhonda in to go over my results. She explained her plan to him to get me to the United States for further treatment. Although he understood our desire to exit Nassau immediately—and he did not blame us for wanting to go—he said it would be bad medicine to let me leave the hospital with no treatment. He assessed that I was in crucial need of surgery since I had obliterated a few discs and damaged my spinal cord. He needed to stabilize my neck. He believed that my chances of any recovery, especially the possibility of ever walking, would be impeded by not having the surgery immediately.

He fought for our trust. He gave Rhonda his phone number and told her to Google him to understand his reputation as a surgeon who had performed many of these surgeries. He used humor, telling us not to worry about his fee because we could never afford him anyway. He assured us he would argue with our insurance company, not us, after the surgery.

We had to decide but felt the need for advice from someone outside of that hospital. We were in a foreign country and did not feel comfortable saying yes to this without more counsel. We were confused and desperate. Rhonda and I both remembered being seated with a doctor, who practiced in Florida, at dinner the night before on the cruise. He was a friendly guy that talked freely about his profession. Rhonda quickly called Hope, who had returned to the ship, and gave her the details of my injuries, including the surgeon's recommendations. Rhonda asked Hope to find the doctor and get his insight. Rhonda spoke with him, and without hesitation, he said that I should have the surgery. He also told her to refuse to pay any more money up front and to tell the hospital to bill us.

On his recommendation, Rhonda called the neurosurgeon and asked him to do the surgery, and we began mentally preparing ourselves. However, hours passed, and we still hadn't heard a word of when the surgery would be performed. When the surgeon came back into the room, I assumed it was time to go, but he had only come to tell us the hospital didn't have the needed medical hardware to put in my neck and they would have to locate it to proceed. He said he "had a guy" who would get it, and he would let us know when he secured the part. That struck me as funny. I could just picture the scene as if it were in a movie — this guy pulling up behind the hospital, opening his trunk, reaching in, and handing the surgeon some sort of an object — an illegal deal made in a back alley to save my life.

Hours ticked by until finally, the part arrived. We prayed, preparing ourselves for whatever happened, and I tried not to panic. My mind was spinning as we waited for them to wheel me away, but then the doctor came back and said the anesthesiologist wasn't there, so he needed to delay surgery. He told us he would only work with one particular anesthesiologist because she was that good.

So, we waited. And waited.

During that wait, the neurosurgeon came back in again with more bad news. He said he had just heard about my heart valve replacement, and he could not do surgery because it was too dangerous. WHAT? We were stunned. We did not understand how he could insist on surgery hours before, yet he was not aware of my medical history. How could he not know until that moment of my heart surgery? I have a scar that looks like a zipper up my chest that is obviously a surgery scar, not to mention we had explained my heart issues during the initial hospital assessment. Our trust was swiftly decreasing.

The rollercoaster of emotions was too much at this point. We had agonized over the decision to get treatment in this horrible hospital based on his assessment that I probably wouldn't live without it, and suddenly, he wasn't going to do the surgery. We were out of options. We were left alone in a room with no information and no idea what would happen. Hours later, the surgeon came in and out of the room several times to look at my chart and me without speaking. Finally, he told us he would talk to his anesthesiologist to get her opinion. We waited. When he came back, he said that they would do surgery in thirty minutes.

The clock read 12:30 am. The place was desolate. Rhonda and I were left completely alone in a dimly lit area waiting for them to take me. We reassured each other that everything would be fine. Occasionally, a random person walked by, looking past us. Finally, a guy came to take me to surgery, leaving Rhonda, still in her swimsuit, alone with just her fear. The guy maneuvered me down a hallway and through some plastic strips covering a doorway, the type used in commercial refrigerated meat coolers. By pushing me through that bizarre curtain, he had delivered me to the operating room.

From my vantage point, all I could see was filth and cobwebs. The ceiling tiles were damaged and water stained. It was like a scene from a 1960s B-rated horror film. I heard my voice in my mind saying, WHAT DID I JUST OKAY?

I had no idea how risky the surgery was when I went under anesthesia. I was still in shock from the accident. My surgeon's conversation gave me hope that surgery would succeed. I didn't understand a minor wrong move could give me an entirely different outcome. I didn't think about the fact that I could die in surgery. I was out of surgery around 4:30 am when my neurosurgeon spoke to Rhonda about the procedure. He told her there was a major fracture and he had removed two discs. He then stabilized my vertebrae by attaching a metal component to secure movement. The surgeon explained that the two discs were up high, under my mandible. With my neck being so short, it was all difficult to access. Without hesitation, he said it was the most difficult he's performed out of the seven thousand. I am so thankful for this extremely talented and compassionate doctor; he was a Godsend.

I woke up in the intensive care unit and the hospital staff eventually brought Rhonda into the room. A nurse suctioned my throat because I couldn't swallow on my own, and saliva would build up, causing me to choke. Much later, after returning to Ohio, I learned this was due to the spinal cord injury and my paralysis. I remember Rhonda asking if I was in pain. My response, "I have no pain at all, but I am hot." Very hot!

I had an infection raging in my body causing a fever. My attending nurses said they had to lower my body temperature, so they turned down the thermostat in the room until it was frigid.

Poor Rhonda was still in her bathing suit with just Hope's hoodie to keep her warm. She was shaking as she made calls to the American Embassy. Rhonda explained what had happened up to this point and asked for information on how to get me out of the Bahamas and flown back to the United States. The conversation was frustrating because the embassy representative thought Rhonda wanted money when all she was requesting was information on how to get to the United States. Eventually, she gave her a list of a dozen companies that could transport me, but she gave no other support or information. Rhonda was on her own. She chose the first company that grabbed her attention, "Fly Reva." Reva was her grandmother's name, so it was familiar. We laugh now that it was probably not the way you want to choose a company that's potentially going to save your life, but at the time, it was a comfort! For a mere $20,000, they would transport me to Cleveland. Things were looking positive. I was alive and we were set to go to the Cleveland Clinic. Well, we thought we were set until the hospital sent word they did not have a bed for me. Fly Reva couldn't transport me without a predetermined hospital acceptance. They offered to take me to Miami for $10,000, suggesting I choose a hospital there. Rhonda tried Broward County and Miami hospitals, but none had any openings that would accept my level of injury. After receiving this news, we knew there was no question about hospitals. I needed to get to the Cleveland Clinic.

The Cleveland Clinic is not only consistently ranked as one of the best hospitals in the United States, but it was also the hospital that helped me through my heart surgery. It is close to home, and home is where I wanted to be. All this played into our decision about which hospital we wanted to be transported to.

It was Thursday morning, approximately 19 hours since my accident. The danger to my life was escalating by the minute.

As we struggled to figure out an alternative plan, the woman from the day before came in to inform us she needed another $20,000 to continue my care. Rhonda told her we couldn't give her any more money and asked her to bill us. This response agitated the woman, and she became angry, sending my nurse, who had been suctioning my throat every few minutes, out of my room. She then told the nurse to hand Rhonda the device, forcing my wife to take over the job so I wouldn't suffocate. The woman and the nurse left the room. Rhonda had no idea how to operate the suctioning machine, but I am very thankful that she figured it out. What a horrible turn of events. The woman returned later in the day only to inform Rhonda she could not stay in my room or anywhere else in the hospital that night.

Growing agitated thinking about leaving me alone in that room, Rhonda begged the woman to let her stay with me. She knew I would die with nobody there to suction my throat. She pleaded with the woman, crying, asking her if she would leave her own husband there to die. The woman calmly stated that it was not company policy to allow her to stay beyond visiting hours even though they let her stay the previous night. No compassion. No concern. She said at 9 pm Rhonda would either have to voluntarily leave the hospital or the police would be called to escort her out. I told her that my wife would not leave my side — as if I had some sort of clout. Rhonda asked to talk to a supervisor. The supervisor restated that Rhonda would have to leave at 9 pm based on company policy. Rhonda kept telling them that they removed the nurse from the room and I would die if she too were made to leave the room. There would be no one there to suction my throat. Silence. They walked out and left us there to figure it out.

Words cannot describe the extreme emotions we experienced that day. We prayed for a miracle as we watched the clock. At 7:30 pm, Fly Reva called to tell us a bed had opened up at the Cleveland Clinic and they were bringing a medical team to get me. They explained that they had to fly in from Fort Lauderdale, so it would be very late and that an ambulance would have to bring us to the plane. Although this was very encouraging news, we agonized and held our breath for the 9 pm deadline, expecting the staff to remove Rhonda from my room, but nobody came.

At 11:30 pm, the life flight arrived, and for the first time in 32 hours, we could exhale. I felt elated as I watched the EMS team move my body from the hospital bed into the ambulance. The 50-minute drive, which should have been about 25 minutes, to the airport was over rough terrain, and it was frightening to be jostled, but the paramedics were kind, and we were relieved to be getting out of Nassau. The ambulance taxied me to the plane and the paramedics lifted me with a sling-like apparatus into the small jet. I was placed on a little bed that was like a shelf. To put this in perspective, Rhonda was sitting at my right foot and a flight nurse sitting in front of her. The pilot was seated just above the right side of my head and the co-pilot was at the left side of my head. It was a small jet. A second flight nurse was at my right side as well, and he suctioned my throat throughout the entire flight.

The moments before take-off were horrible for me. Maybe it resulted from leaving all the fear of the Bahamas behind and finally feeling safe enough to relax a little bit, but every sensation was magnified. The gurgling noise from the suctioning of my throat was awful. I felt agitated as though time was slowing to a stop. It felt like it was an eternity before we lifted off. I was grateful for Rhonda's presence because her calmness kept me from panicking.

We landed in Cleveland 3 ½ hours later at 4:08 am amidst falling snow. We had to be cleared through customs, so Rhonda went with a medic and the pilots while I and the other medic stayed on the plane. This is where Hope and Ron's quick thinking paid off. Without our passports, we would not have left the Bahamas and enter the United States. About a half-hour later, Rhonda returned with paramedics to transport me to the Cleveland Clinic. Our arrival there differed completely from our arrival at the hospital in the Bahamas. The hospital staff moved quickly, running out to move me from the ambulance to the emergency room. They immediately scrubbed my body, horrified at the sand still covering me, cutting off my swim shorts that had not been removed. I could see the concern on their faces I had gone through surgery in this condition. My fever was raging.

The nurses kept apologizing for scrubbing so hard, telling me they were worried about hurting me. I assured them they could scrub away. I could feel nothing.

Even the way my wife was treated was immensely different. A staff member led her away to shower and found clean clothes for her to wear. No one even mentioned money or costs. Their foremost concern was care for both of us.

Vivid images come to me about the differences between the two hospitals, and I am filled with gratitude that I survived the filth of the first operating room and the hospital's conditions. I am deeply grateful for the neurosurgeon who saved my life there.

The Cleveland Clinic quickly assessed that I needed a second surgery to stabilize my neck further. As opposed to the surgeon in the Bahamas, who had entered from the front of my neck for the sake of fusing the C3, C4, and C5 vertebrae, the Cleveland Clinic doctors felt they needed to go in from the back and reinforce my vertebrae from a different angle, fusing C3, C4, C5, and C6. They also found two blood clots in my leg where a vascular surgeon needed to insert an Inferior Vena Cava (IVC) Filter. The Inferior Vena Cava is the largest vein in your body that carries blood from your lower body to your heart and lungs. The IVC filter is inserted in the Inferior Vena Cava to prevent blood clots from moving through your blood and into your lungs. I was back in surgery by Saturday morning, and then things became a fog of hallucinations and pain.

Although the events are a blur, my hallucinations remain vivid from that time. I was in a constant dream state, thinking I needed to work, asking for my laptop. My nurse had to remind me many times where I was and what surgery I had just been through to lead me back to reality gently.

I had a dream that I was Steve Jobs, running a major corporation and that I had a bunch of his grown children working for me. It was so real—as though my headquarters were in the hospital and I was managing it all from my bed. My friend Ron, who had returned from the cruise, spent the night with me so Rhonda could get a little sleep in a nearby hotel. He sat up in a chair, covered in a blanket right beside my bed. I remember him laughing at me because of the wild things I said about us being on a trip in a snowstorm in Alaska. We were looking for my two dogs, Maize and Blue, and had checked ourselves into a hotel room.

Ron knew I was lying there in a hospital bed at the Cleveland Clinic, but apparently, I was convinced we were in a hotel room. It was surreal to have the dual images of knowing the guy who saved my life was staying with me as I recovered from surgery but still having the dream state. It was as though I could perceive the reality, but at the same time, I was seeing a split-screen of a separate life, moving between the dream state and reality.

The hospital had me so sedated with medications I couldn't stay grounded in reality, which was unnerving. I wanted no one to know about the hallucinations because I was afraid they would think I was crazy. When my nurse looked like a cat, like she was in a Halloween costume with a cat face and a cat print nurse's uniform, I tried to act normal until she was whisked up into the ceiling tiles and disappeared. I may have said something abnormal then because she asked me if I was okay, and instantly all was normal, and she was standing right before me looking like a regular person. It was hard to keep up with what was actually happening. Most of the time, I thought my bed was in the gift shop at the beach and I could hear the waves crashing hard on the shore. I saw many people walking through, and I thought they were shopping while I lay on a bed right in the middle of it.

I couldn't wake up from the dream state for the entire week I spent at the Cleveland Clinic, and I was still hallucinating while being transported to MetroHealth Hospital. This hospital is well known for its Level I Adult Trauma Center and its spinal cord rehabilitation. It is where I spent the next three months in the spinal cord injury rehabilitation unit. I'm fortunate my surgeon at the Cleveland Clinic knew this and recommended my transfer there.

Upon my transfer, I thought I could hear all the traffic everywhere in the entire world. Verbalizing this gained a reaction from the paramedics, prompting them to keep asking me if I knew where I was and what was happening. I had no grasp of either thing. I had no idea where I was or what was happening, which led to great anxiety as I transitioned to the rehabilitation hospital. The medication continued to keep me in a state of haziness and confusion.

When I arrived at MetroHealth, I thought I was in a group home. As I lay there, I got very afraid of being alone. My mind could not conceptualize the reality of where I was or what would happen at this facility. Reflecting back in time, it's clear that the pain medications brought on the hallucinations, but I couldn't see that at the time. My thoughts were jumbled, and it was hard to know exactly what was happening as I went between fear and confusion.

As hard as it was, the dream state was much easier than the reality to come. On my first day at MetroHealth, they assessed me as C3, the highest point of my injury on the vertebrae. My ASIA scale impairment was a C, which meant my motor function was incomplete, but I had no motor skills at all at this point. ASIA - American Spinal Injury Association Impairment Scale is used by the rehabilitation team to assess the sensory and motor function levels affected by the spinal cord injury. I could only move my eyes and lips. I felt only despair. Why would Rhonda want to stay with me? I was worthless. It reminded me of the early days of our marriage and how much I had failed her with all the issues we had to overcome with my mother. My hopelessness took me far back into our past, attacking my spirit at the core. I started to believe a story that I had no value, and my old failures were reinforcing those ideas for me and dragging me into a pit of complete darkness. It was as though I was right back in my 20s and had not grown or changed at all. And now I felt powerless to fix it.

CHAPTER 7
Churning Waters

The Past Resurfaces

After Greg's death, we tried to find some level of normal in the middle of our pain and grief. Rhonda was starting her senior year of high school and I was working several jobs in addition to the pizza shop. One of my other jobs was as a caddy. I caddied and bussed tables at a country club, trying to save money and figure out my future plans. Rhonda has little memory of that year because of the level of traumatic shock she experienced. We know a lot more today about post-traumatic stress disorder (PTSD) and the toll it can take on a person, but back then, we just tried to get through the days. The trauma of Greg's death affected the entire family and changed their lives in both subtle and profound ways.

In June of 1982, Rhonda graduated high school; I proposed and she accepted. We were married the following May and positive things started happening for us. I worked in Rhonda's uncle's machine shop making a better wage than my prior jobs and were happy together. I also thought I was managing the issues in my family pretty well. I felt lucky and blessed to start a whole new chapter and anticipated accomplishing all the plans we had set out to achieve. I hoped things in my family would stay calm.

Unfortunately, they did not stay calm at all. During the first year of our marriage, my mom attempted suicide again. This horrible event took place on a day I had planned to visit. She knew exactly what time I was getting off work and that I was on my way over to visit her. It was hard on me to be the one who walked in on her, and my intense reaction was based on years of similar experiences. I had witnessed her other suicide attempts during my childhood when I was a preteen, and I wanted to believe we were past all those issues. We were not. On this day, which was supposed to be just a nice visit, I pulled up to the house, walked to her door, and knocked. No answer. I grabbed the door handle, turned the knob and it opened. There she was, sitting on a chair slumped over the kitchen stove. I could hear the gas hissing, but no burner lit. Since I could not smell gas in the room, it was not clear if it was truly a suicide attempt or staged. At the moment, you react to what you see. When you have time to reflect, some instances, such as this one, become clearer. I was trapped in my emotions, and she needed help that I was not equipped to give her. I needed the help as well, and I called a psychiatrist in our city to ask what I could do because my mother refused to go to the hospital that night. I spent hours talking with her until she convinced me she was okay and past her suicidal feelings. I told him over the phone what had happened and her history. He thought this was staged. He told me it sounded like she was searching for attention and that most people who try suicide would not stage something, they just do it. I was young, but I was searching for answers. I'm glad I reached out because it gave me an understanding of why she might do something like this—it was her way of crying for help!

My dad also attempted suicide when I was young by taking a bottle of sleeping pills after my mom asked for the divorce. I remember an ambulance and a few police officers coming to the house and the fear that my father would die. I guess it scared my mom, too, because she agreed to a year of counseling with him when he left the hospital. In retrospect, I can see how chaos, guilt, and manipulation were normal to my parents. My siblings and I were tossed around in the ensuing emotional storm, developing interactional patterns that were not healthy.

When I found my mom in that kitchen, not knowing if she was dead or alive, it exposed those unhealthy patterns in me, but I couldn't totally see them yet. Rhonda's clarity of thought regarding my mom was difficult for me to understand because of my lifelong conditioning. Guilt and fear kept me from seeing my mother's manipulations for what they were. Rhonda had always respected my relationship with my mother but saw the dysfunction. This was never doubted on my part. She witnessed my interactions with my mother firsthand and would point out the manipulation. Even though we were young, Rhonda was wise to my mother's patterns. She would say, "John, your mom is trying to make you feel bad about this situation to get her way." I knew that Rhonda had never experienced this dynamic in her family to know the difference.

I didn't see the signs. I worked hard to meet my mom's demands without affecting Rhonda. It was seriously challenging. I learned to shield Rhonda as much as I could because I was entangled in my mom's drama and it was draining me, and I could not find a way out. Arguing with Rhonda over my mom would cause more stress even though she was trying to help me. It caused a lot of friction in our marriage.

Before we had kids, I could balance my mom's demands well enough to avoid major damage to our marriage. I was emotionally exhausted, but I handled it. After our kids, Brandon and Jordyn, were born, it became much more difficult. Between work, spending time with my family, and dealing with my mom, I was worn down. By the time Jordyn, our youngest child, was born, my mom wanted to see the kids alone and we could never allow it. After witnessing the unhealthy relationships between my mother and her own children, Rhonda did not trust her, which led to my frustrations. Her manipulation grew. My guilt grew. Problems crept into our marriage because I couldn't break free from my mom.

One night our argument about my mother pushed me to a breaking point, and I decided that I could not argue about her anymore. I did not want to go to bed angry again in our house, so I called a friend and asked if I could stay at his house for the night. Leaving our house was one of the worst mistakes I made in our marriage because I decided in anger to just escape instead of trying to talk through our issues. At that moment, I was sick of conflict. I am not proud of that decision and would change every moment of it if I could. It shook me up to sleep that one night away from home and made me realize what was important. I knew that I was not putting my family first, and I wanted that more than anything. I wanted to be the man they deserved for me to be. My main priority was to my wife and children, and that night away helped me see what I could lose if I did not show them just how important they were to me. My actions had not made that loyalty clear, so my task became clear to me. Go home and work it out and that's what I did.

Rhonda was able to put up a block and not let my mom control her. It was impossible for me to do so. My mom grew up in a difficult period in Germany with a single mother raising her and her siblings in a war-torn country. My mother would always bring up the fact that her mother would have the same response to our particular situation when she was a young girl, and it was harsh. It was always followed up with her saying we must not love her enough or we wouldn't act that way. Her guilt-inducing comments controlled me. I felt trapped in a no-win situation.

Maybe the good memories I had of my mom caused my blind spot. I always knew she loved me, and I saw her compassion toward people and animals. Two prime examples of this come to my mind as positive memories of her. The first one happened one day when my mother was shopping in our city and an elderly man collapsed on the sidewalk in front of a bank. A crowd of bystanders was forming around him and his wife as she came upon the scene. His skin changed color and he wasn't breathing. This was years before cell phones, so someone from the crowd went to call for an emergency unit. My mother, who was never trained at CPR (Cardio-pulmonary Resuscitation) and had only seen it performed on television, jumped into action to try and resuscitate him. She continued until the emergency team arrived and they thanked her. The man did not live, but the Governor of Michigan gave my mom an award for her heroism. She was upset he hadn't lived and spoke with passion about it for many years.

The second event was when my mother was driving on a remarkably busy road when she spotted a small rabbit in the opposite lane. She pulled her car to the side of the road, exited her vehicle, and witnessed no cars slowing down to help. Instead, they were driving over the top of this bunny luckily too frightened to move. My mother walked into the road, slowed down the traffic, and saved the rabbit. Her compassion for animals was evident as she risked her life to save a bunny's life.

I respected how hard she worked to keep our family together. We always had food, shelter, and clean clothes. Times were hard for her and she was frugal and fought to keep her kids, even though she was also psychologically and physically abusive to us. It was confusing. I wanted to believe she would be good with our kids. I wanted them to know the good parts of their grandma. Rhonda found it strange that she wanted to be with the kids alone and explicitly forbade my mom from seeing them without one of us present. Her wisdom was an important part of me breaking free from the situation, but it took years and it created distance between us as husband and wife. Although the topic of my mom's character was not a black and white conversation, the safety of our children was.

Our early years of marriage were also hindered by my hatred for my dad still simmering under the surface. From the time I found out about the abuse, I felt a need to confront him. I wanted justice. The hurt was deep.

The simmer turned back into a boil one night when Rhonda and I went to dinner at a cozy little restaurant. We walked through the door, and there, sitting at the bar, was my father. He and a few others at the bar turned to see who was walking through the door, which made me instantly think he was a regular at this establishment. I honestly did not know what to say or do as we made eye contact.

Although it had been years since I last saw him, I am the spitting image of my father, so there was no doubting who he was. Deciding to stay, we were seated by the hostess. The restaurant was small, making this encounter awkward and uncomfortable. Before we had an opportunity to order our dinner, my father made a rude comment in our direction. I heard him say loudly, "Can you believe what the cat drug in here?" I could feel the pressure as the anger bubbled up inside me. I wanted to yell at him and say, "How dare you say anything to me when you chose to abandon your children after a divorce. How dare you say anything after having abused your stepdaughter, who you adopted." I wanted to say so much to him about all that he had done to his children over the years, but I didn't. I respected our surroundings and didn't want to create a scene. We stood up and walked out. I mentally punched the wall as adrenaline flooded my body.

Around the same time, a friend of my younger sister Mary Ann called her to tell her she had seen my dad at a wedding, and he was saying terrible things about her and my other sisters. She said that he was attacking their character by saying they had been with many men. The allegations were lies. Mary Ann shared this with me because of the hurtful words used. She needed someone to listen, someone who could understand the pain it caused. Hearing about this, I was furious. How could he continue to intentionally hurt us after all these years?

The gossip pushed me over the edge. I had to confront him for spreading rumors about my sisters. I decided to drive to his home and make him aware that I wouldn't allow him to disrespect them. I knocked and Donna answered the door. She invited me in, but I decided to stay outside. I asked for my father and she went back inside to ask him to come talk with me. He opened the door, saying hello, but I wasn't there for pleasantries. After all these years, I first began to ask why he would continue the hatred, telling him what I had heard. I said, "I won't allow you to hurt us any longer, so go on with your life and leave us alone." He just looked at me with no feeling in his expression, first denying it and then with anger in his voice, saying that he could say whatever he wanted. He gave me no answers. He had no remorse. He had nothing to say to me, nothing at all. At that moment, intense rage filled my soul. I walked away, not knowing what I would have done had it escalated.

After that confrontation, the hatred consumed me, and I had nowhere to direct it. I was drinking too much and didn't stop until our first child, Brandon, was born. Having children settled me down and helped me to focus on the important issues in life. Although the drama with my mom increased and became more intense, I realized that I had too many responsibilities and that I needed to stay level-headed. After all, I had witnessed this type of behavior throughout my life, it wasn't something new. It was time to stand up and change this cycle of events. It saddens me to know I should have been stronger earlier when it was just Rhonda and me, but I'm grateful that having Brandon and Jordyn, helped me to see the role I had in making a change in our family dynamic.

About eight years had passed since that last encounter with my father when I was Christmas shopping with some friends and ran into my cousin, Susan. She told me my dad was sick with emphysema amongst other ailments and may not live much longer. This new information was unsettling and made me think about my situation. I had gone through years of heartache without him. My entire life replayed in my head, all the good and bad times, as Susan and I stood there talking. Did I really want my father to die without me speaking to him again? I still wanted answers. I wanted to give him one last chance to be the father I thought he was when I was a child. Like my mom, I hoped he was not all bad. I hoped there were good parts of him that were still there, and I needed to know if it was true. Although it was difficult for me, I decided to call him.

I let him know I was calling because I had heard about his bad health and asked if he would tell me all that was wrong. Our talk was a bit awkward at first. We muddled through some formalities, but eventually, my father asked if my family and I would be willing to come for dinner to get reacquainted. After talking with Rhonda, I accepted the invitation, and we went to dinner. For the first time, he met my wife, our son, Brandon, who was four and a half years old, and our newborn daughter, Jordyn. I felt like I was meeting him for the first time as well. It had been so many years since I had seen him, and I didn't really know him. We were all nervous at first, but that soon passed because my dad and his wife Donna made us feel very welcome in their home.

That dinner was a new beginning and the start of many more visits. That night my dad expressed how sorry he was for the way things turned out, which was the turning point of our reconciliation. I didn't forget the past, and I don't believe you have to, but I did learn to forgive. My dad's health cycled for the next eleven years, improving and declining. As time passed, we spent more time together, with many family gatherings, including my step-siblings and their children. Eventually, we all became comfortable with one another, and that's when the difficulty happened. My dad and Donna invited our children to stay the night as their other grandchildren had. Most parents love to have their kids stay the night with their grandparents, but our children didn't know what we knew, and my dad didn't know what I knew.

Here I was back in the predicament of having to say no to a parent, but this time there was no question in my mind about the safety of my children. We made an excuse each time the subject came up as to why it wouldn't work. Each time the answer was no. The requests became more frequent, so I knew what needed to be done. I was compelled to tell my father why I could not leave Brandon and Jordyn with him.

One nice summer day when we went for a visit, I asked Rhonda and Donna if they would take the kids to the community pool so my dad and I could talk in private. I dreaded this conversation, but here we were, just the two of us, and it had to happen. I started by explaining how difficult this was for me to say but that I had to get it out into the open. I told him that he kept asking to watch my children either for the day or overnight and that I couldn't let him because I knew what happened with him and my sister, and I could never allow him to be alone with my children. At first, he denied abusing my sister, but then he admitted that he had inappropriately touched her. He broke down and said he felt horrible about what he did to her. His story was different from that of my mom and sister, who said it had happened many times, and he said it was an isolated incident. It didn't matter because once is one too many times to hurt a child. He had every excuse imaginable and promised it would never happen again, but I still couldn't leave the kids alone with him.

I was overwhelmed that my dad finally admitted that he caused the divorce and had abused my sister. It helped me begin to trust him to tell me the truth about our lives but not to be alone with our kids. That topic was off the table permanently. The feeling of hatred stopped boiling in my chest when he apologized at that first dinner, and his admission of guilt and his attempt to make things right when I confronted him helped the anger to dissipate finally. I had survived and was beginning to heal some of the emotional wounds from my childhood.

CHAPTER 8
Faith

"Only in the darkness can you see the stars."

— Martin Luther King Jr.

F aith is an interesting word. I was trying to have faith in my dad, in myself, and in my ability to protect my family. I was looking around for cues to tell me what to do. I was young, yet I knew that I wanted my life to look a certain way. I wanted peace in my home and for my family and to know they were always safe. I was looking for my path and what would help me to feel secure in the future. I see now how I had worked so hard after my dad left to find some solid ground. I was searching for a way to be okay, which always led me back to the one thing that made me feel centered and that was baseball.

After high school, I had to look harder to find opportunities to play baseball, but I always found them. It's funny how playing ball provided a sense of security. Baseball, the thing I enjoyed so much early in life, did help me stay grounded in adulthood. It helped me stay on course. Baseball was my thing, my true north. It was a constant in my childhood, and as I grew older, that continued. I know it's just a game, something that people do for enjoyment, but it's been my refuge. Maybe this is why I often dream about the game. Many of those dreams have evoked images of me as a young boy or as an adult hitting the ball as it is pitched across the plate, stealing bases, or diving for a line drive. In some of my dreams, I experienced the clichés of hitting the game-winning home run or catching the deep fly ball up against the fence to end the game. All those images felt solid, as though they were connecting me to myself. From playing in the streets and on vacant land in my neighborhood to actual organized league games on well-groomed diamonds, baseball gave me something solid I could count on, whether in reality or from my dreams.

After high school, softball, directly and indirectly, provided stability for me as well. I joined a church softball league which then required me to go to two church services a month. I would not have chosen to go to church that often without softball, so the league forced me to meet those requirements. These requirements led to my meeting of some wonderful, loving people at a Nazarene church, and my mind began to expand to consider issues of faith and the meaning of life.

I grew up Catholic and attended a Catholic school, up until the divorce was final. It was too expensive keeping us children enrolled. My mom made sure we went to mass when she was still mentally sound and in our home. As everything disintegrated in our family, attending church was not a strong enough force to hold my interest, so I didn't go on my own. I just was not compelled to find my spiritual path, but if the opportunity presented itself, I would go to church. I attended a Baptist church with an old girlfriend and occasionally went with my family, but while in high school, a life of faith did not interest me.

Although I was not seeking it, attending the Nazarene church, which was associated with my softball team, exposed me to a faith community, and I began to understand what a life based on faith looked like. I was not influenced by their rules or doctrine as much as by how they lived. My understanding of faith came from the examples I saw in people. One of the main people who affected me was my friend, Carl. Our friendship started on the softball field and expanded into other areas of our lives. We were constantly together and became remarkably close friends. His girlfriend, Debbie, and Rhonda also became friends, and we were best man and maid of honor at their wedding.

It's hard to explain how Carl's friendship has affected me over the years except to say that his example of spirituality has been a constant encouragement. When I helped Carl and Debbie move to Ohio after their wedding, I hoped that one day we could move there too, and we eventually did. Now we only live 45 minutes away from each other and that connection continues. During my time in the hospital, Carl's gifts were so special because they came from our shared history of sports. He has helped with so many home projects and always knows what I need to hear. I'm amazed at how meeting him through church has helped to shape my life.

Carl was one of many people at the church who influenced me. In that group, I saw a pattern of devotion to family, the community, and to God that was new to me. There were two other men, in particular, that stand out in my memory: my coach, Al and his assistant, Gordy, who happened to be Debbie's father. They revealed their faith by showing me grace. Always teaching and taking an interest in my life, they filled in for the father I was missing. This happened when I needed it the most, and it helped me develop strong, healthy relationships.

I was dealing with a lot of questions about death in the back of my mind, and I still had that simmering hatred toward my dad and ambivalence regarding my mom. These painful thoughts sometimes came to the surface, but I tried to push them down and go on with life. The older I became, the harder it was to ignore the thoughts. I needed help to make sense of it all. Because of my softball team's requirement to attend church, seeds of faith were being planted that eventually became particularly important to me as I sorted out these painful areas of my life.

Rhonda's family was involved in their small community church, and often, I attended with her as well. Rhonda and I were married in that church and grew close to many members, especially couples around our age. As the years passed and our children were born, and we were able to grow closer through sharing our life experiences. Our church members shared in our joys and helped us when we had no idea how we would survive. They became more than people we fellowshipped with in a church building; they became a part of our family.

I also developed a common bond with a handful of men from the church through working on home projects, playing volleyball, and having family and couples outings. I had taken up the sport of target shooting with a compound bow and learned that some of these men had the same interest since they were all hunters. Our house sat on three and a half acres of property surrounded by dense woods, so it was an ideal place for us to practice our target shooting skills. In the fall, we often set up deer targets—bull's eyes and bales of straw with balloons attached—and we would gather to practice shooting. It was always entertaining when one of us missed a target completely. First, there would be laughter and then the friendly chiding followed while we all searched for the errant arrow we would finally find buried under the leaves. I loved the competitive spirit and the fun of spending time with these men.

When deer hunting season came, I was fortunate to get invited to join in the yearly ritual of going "up north" with Jack, Ken, and Larry to hunt for five or six days. This was the first time in my life I would go bow hunting and I had no idea what to expect. After leaving work, we packed a camper, drove 10 hours to the Upper Peninsula of Michigan, and arrived in complete darkness to set up camp. The group's goal was to hunt and harvest a deer, but for me, the time spent in camp, sharing meals, telling funny stories with the guys, and enjoying the woods' natural beauty was what I enjoyed the most. It was something I looked forward to each year.

On one trip, I had a major life-defining experience. It was our last day in camp and not one of us had shot a deer. We all headed in separate directions for our morning hunt. It was understood that everyone would finish hunting by noon, tear down their stands, return to camp, pack up and begin the long trek home. It was a brilliant, sunny morning as I sat high in a tree on my deer stand. I could not have imagined a more vivid landscape than the one I experienced that morning.

My senses were heightened by the sounds, smells, and beauty that were all around me. The sun glistened through the bare trees that shed red, brown and yellow leaves to the forest floor beneath me. The leaves that blanketed the ground must have been two to three inches thick. I loved the fresh, crisp morning air, mixed with the aroma of the tall pine tree I had perched in. The woods surrounding me were so alive with a multitude of birds chirping and the sound of squirrels snapping twigs and rustling through the colorful leaves on the ground. It was invigorating!

When you sit in a tree stand in the middle of the woods, you have ample time to be quiet with your thoughts. As I sat there high above the forest floor, my thoughts wandered to a deeper question about my very existence. It was as if I was replaying snippets of my life from the beginning to that moment sitting in a tree stand. I was thinking to myself, "What is the purpose of life and death? Are we born just to die? Is this all there is to our existence?" I felt oddly exhilarated sitting in the quiet tree stand as things came into focus for me. I felt connected to a greater purpose and a greater being than myself, which felt like a connection to God. There was some deep thinking to my questions.

I sat there praying and asking God to help me understand my thoughts when suddenly, a deer walked out into the clearing. I stood, waited for the perfect moment, pulled back the string of my bow, lined up the shot, and let the arrow fly. I had the first deer of my hunting career and my last, but the real thing I walked away with was that intense feeling of connection to something bigger than myself.

Everyone has their own spiritual path, and as I close this chapter, I want to be clear that my intention is not to put my beliefs on anyone else. Following my spinal cord accident, I wrestled with questions based on my understanding of God. We all have questions based on our belief systems, and so understanding my background is important to the rest of the story.

After my spinal cord injury, my questions were broad, ranging from wondering if God was punishing me for something I did wrong to wondering if everything in our lives was just by chance. I had found comfort in the feeling of God's presence in the woods all those years ago, and that comfort gave me strength.

I felt a connection to everything around me, and the loving presence I felt in that moment.

CHAPTER 9

Thick Fog Hanging over Rough Waters

Lying in that hospital bed at the Cleveland Clinic, my thoughts wandered back to my hunting trip in the Upper Peninsula of Michigan. I couldn't help but think about that deer and how feeling that God was part of that experience had become vital to me in so many ways. At this point in my journey, the deer was back in the woods and my mind was clouded with doubts. Where was God in all this terrible mess? As terrifying as the hallucinations were, I was unprepared for the despair about to hit.

During the first few days at MetroHealth Rehabilitation Hospital, I began to think more clearly, but that clarity was frightening. As the hallucinations disappeared, self-doubt emerged and overtook me. It was at this moment when I understood the dire state of my situation: total paralysis. Staring straight up at the ceiling tiles, with a big brace on my neck, not able to swallow water on my own, and a feeding tube down my throat. There was a tube close to my lips that fished its way to a box on a pole next to my bed. A nurse explained that the tube-controlled lights in the room, the television on and off, volume control and calling for assistance to the nurses' station. All this was done by either sucking in or blowing into the tube. I felt lost.

I slowly came out of the cloud and back into the reality of my life as it was. As I lay in a hospital bed feeling lifeless, I wondered what good I was to anyone? My mind was flooded with questions. How could I work? How would I get paid? How would I do all the work around the house? Who would take care of our vehicle upkeep? Would I ever play baseball again? Would I ever ride a bike again? Would I ever cut into a steak again or be able to bring a fork up to my mouth? The questions were endless and just kept swirling through my mind. It was becoming clear that I could not support my family because I couldn't even turn my head, let alone move any other part of my body. I was sure Rhonda would leave me. Why would she stay?

As the days passed, I sank deeper into myself. It felt as though I were surrounded by fog. I saw no hope. No way to be useful to anyone. I Had No Way Out! Two questions consumed my thoughts: What is my purpose? And is my wife going to leave me? I had no answer to the first question, but I was sure that Rhonda would leave me. I saw myself as a person locked inside the shell of my body. My past coping skills were of no use at this point. I couldn't confront paralysis like I had confronted my dad.

I couldn't help anyone with anything. I couldn't even scratch my own nose. I was quickly introduced to the harsh emotion that people who become disabled often feel — despair.

By the second day at MetroHealth, Rhonda's humor saved me. It was the day I fell to my lowest point and couldn't take it anymore. Rhonda had entered my room, hugged me, kissed me, and asked me how I was doing today. I asked her to sit down on the edge of the bed. We were alone with no distractions. She had no idea what the next thing coming out of my mouth would be, but I'm sure she sensed something. Looking at her, I finally asked her if she was planning to leave me.

"Leave you! Why would I leave you? You were too hard to train in the first place!" she said with a laugh that was both comforting and funny at the same time. I loved it!

Her reaction brought out the laughter of relief for me. She could not believe I would even consider her leaving me. She didn't even take the idea seriously.

Her words snapped me out of the haze that seemed inescapable and gave me a reason to live. Before that conversation, I had felt inadequate and undeserving of her. She is my rock. The fog lifted as I saw the truth that my wife was not with me for what I could do for her but because she loved me. To her, that was never a question.

Once I felt secure with Rhonda, the question of purpose needed to be answered. What was my purpose?

As a young man, I saw my worth like most people do in relation to what I could do for other people. Earning a living and taking care of my home and my family was particularly important to me. As I began the rehabilitation process, I had to rely on other people for everything. I depended completely on people for every need. It is impossible to describe the humbling effect of having to ask someone to scratch your nose, give you a sip of water, or administer your new bowel movement routine. I cannot explain what my support system of family, friends, and caregivers meant to me during those first weeks but also beyond those days. I went from being a guy who wanted to do everything I could for others to a guy who could do absolutely nothing for himself, let alone for other people.

Rhonda's words gave me my life back, and the staff at MetroHealth helped to give me the courage to live that life again. I don't think we often allow words we hear from other people to sink in and take hold when they need to be heard and understood the most. I am just thankful that I allowed those words Rhonda conveyed to sink in and make a difference in the most difficult time of my life, at the exact time I needed to hear it. What a gift!

As the saying goes, good things seem to come in threes, and my third gift was a guy named Rich who came rolling into my room in his wheelchair. It was nearing the end of my fourth day and Rhonda had gone home for the night. He introduced himself, explaining that his paralysis resulted from an infection. Laughing, he asked me, "What are you in for?" as though we were in prison. Not that I know what it's like to be in prison, I have never been there. I did feel like a prisoner, though, locked inside of myself with no way out, and Rich's humor gave me a spark to jumpstart that person into action that was trapped inside of me. His words helped me understand that I was not alone in this hospital or alone with the challenges in front of me.

Soon I would meet more friends, like John and his wife Linda, who became particularly important to me in my recovery process. A wave also injured John, so having him to talk to was very impactful. We had a shared experience of being on a wonderful vacation and then suddenly losing our physical abilities. Rhonda and I frequently visited John and Linda in one of the hospital's common areas, and at times we would share food or a story. John sustained an injury leaving him as a paraplegic, so he soon found his way to my room, wheeling himself down the hallways. I enjoyed getting to know his funny wit. Rich, John, and I developed a special bond, and the staff noticed and started referring to us as the three amigos. As odd as it may sound, it gave me an identity.

Having these new friends helped me begin engaging with my family and friends, and I began chipping away at the shell of despair that had encased me. I saw that one thing I could do—a purpose—was to spread the humor. It became evident early that I needed humor to jumpstart my life again, so I decided to be upbeat and use levity to help other people, and that was certainly the beginning of helping myself. My sense of humor was one thing that I had liked about myself and was still there. My desire to be a positive person and encourage people was also something I liked about myself. I still could encourage others, and I wanted to access that part of me again.

So, there it was, I had my wife, and I had a purpose I expanded to a broader way of thinking. I always loved people without condition and enjoyed being social. I needed to harness that love for people to help myself stay positive. Every day, friends and family would come to be with me, and I felt that love and kindness, but I felt so lonely when they left. This was a daily struggle, one that I didn't see changing. It was easy to fixate on insecurity or loss, so I had to change my mindset to realize this was much bigger than just myself. I needed to focus on my purpose of being a positive person for myself and others to keep going, and most important, engage in therapy. I had to train my brain and my body to stay positive and fight for recovery. This was not an easy thing to do with so much uncertainty, no mobility, and little hope. I knew I had to change my mindset.

My daily therapy schedule started with an SLP (speech-language pathologist) because I needed to relearn the skill of swallowing. Having a feeding tube through my nose and down my throat was beyond annoying and needed to go away. That was followed by occupational therapy because I had no arm or hand function; it was essential to keep them in motion. It ended with physical therapy to keep the legs and feet moving and retraining all those mid to lower half functions. This happened five days a week, three and a half to four and a half hours a day.

Initially, therapy was not only extremely challenging but also very frightening for me. I was uncertain about what to expect. At the onset, I always had the feeling I would fall out of my wheelchair, especially when I was being moved to a mat table or my hospital bed. I had to force myself to trust those helping me, and I had to decide to take advantage of every possibility that I was given.

> *"The greatest danger for most of us is not that our aim is too high and we miss it, but that it is too low and we reach it."*
> *– Michelangelo*

If the physical therapist or occupational therapist asked me to do something, I would try to do it to the best of my abilities. None of this was easy since I had to put all my trust in these people I did not know.

The rehabilitation process challenged me in many ways, mentally and physically. Rhonda had to go back to work and did not want me to be alone, so she and our friend Hope designed a schedule so someone was with me every single day during the three months I was at MetroHealth. They worked out the schedule and people took vacation days from their jobs, so I was never alone. Although I appreciated the support, honestly, some days, it was mentally draining for me. There were periods I just wanted to be by myself. When you are in the depths of depression, it is incredibly taxing when all you want to do is crawl into your own mind and hide. You are trying to sort things out in your head, but you also feel like you need to stay engaged in conversation. In retrospect, however, that support system was a critical part of my recovery. I had dozens of friends and family there over those months praying for me and supporting me. I had to stay upbeat for them and myself. The other patients on my floor and the staff also needed me to show up and be the positive person I was designed to be.

From the moment the fog lifted at MetroHealth, I knew this was a facility with some of the most caring professionals I had ever experienced in my life. They have left a lasting impression I will never forget. The first week was spent learning the staff on all the shifts and what my routine would be like. They were certainly all unique individuals, but they shared the same purpose and goals, which was to attend to my needs so I could focus on recovery. From the doctors, nurses, and therapists to the cleaning staff, I was always treated with respect and care. This was extremely important since I was in a very fragile state, physically and emotionally.

On the first day at MetroHealth, we met with my doctor and he began by explaining his thoughts on the severity of my injury. He talked about paralysis, the facility, therapy, and how things worked at this rehabilitation hospital. The biggest thing that stuck with me, and I can still hear him say, was, "Therapy will be extensive and hard at times, but with a positive attitude and commitment to do what is asked, you never know what can come back."

It was difficult for me to understand how I was supposed to work hard when there was no mobility in my body, none! I had this odd feeling that my body was encased in a block of cement from my neck down to my toes. This was more like a mental sensation and not what I could actually feel. I could not see my body since they had me lying flat on my back. They did this because it is difficult to regulate blood pressure in patients with a spinal cord injury, so my bed's head was tilted up slowly each day to ensure that my blood pressure did not bottom out, causing me to pass out. Compression hose and ace wrappings encompassed my legs from toes to hips. I also had an elastic abdominal binder wrapped around my torso, which helped with my blood pressure too.

I spent the first days staring at the ceiling, having to lie flat on my back. Oddly, high above me was a backlit ceiling tile with an image of a sandy beach with rolling waves in the background. It was beautiful but obviously due to my injury's nature, not something I wished to stare at for the next three months. A few days later, I was returned to my room after therapy and it was gone, changed out with another tile. I never mentioned that to anyone on the staff, but I'm sure someone had known about my accident and realized the ceiling tile would be a constant trigger. I was thankful for the hospital's willingness to do this for me, even though it might seem trivial to some people. The gesture showed me they cared about my feelings and emotional wellbeing.

During those first weeks, I often apologized to the staff when they attended to me. I guess it was my weird way of coping. They always responded by gently reminding me I could not do these tasks myself and saying I didn't need to apologize to them for doing their jobs. Their response to my vulnerability eroded the wall of my insecurities and I began to trust them.

Being paralyzed affects more than a person's extremities. A spinal cord injury almost always affects control over the bladder and bowel. This disconnect occurs because the nerves controlling these internal organs are attached to the spinal cord's base and then pass down through the cauda equina, referred to as "the horse's tail." Messages are no longer passed from the nerves in the bladder and bowel to the brain. When this occurs, a catheter and suppository are used, so these vital organs are voided or emptied.

I cannot begin to explain how difficult it is emotionally to have someone you do not know administer these things for you. Your personal space is no longer personal and must be relinquished to your caregiver. You lose all sense of privacy. One night I was given a suppository for my daily bowel routine to void. I fell asleep before it took effect. I woke up sometime later and thought I saw a large figure in my room. As I became more conscious, I realized it was a male nurse, and I asked him why he was in my room. He said, "Go back to sleep, I have already changed you." What? I did not know he had been there. He laughed and said, "I've taken care of it." His humor made the uncomfortable things easier. These types of interactions became an integral part of developing the trust necessary for my recovery.

CHAPTER 10
What Next?

April 24, 2013, about two and a half weeks into my time at MetroHealth, we participated in what is known as the family meeting. It felt like an intervention like the ones I had watched on television. My doctor, main nurse, therapists, social worker, immediate family, in-laws, sister-in-law, and our friends, Ron and Hope, all participated in the meeting. The only things missing from this equation were the cameras from a major television network recording it for broadcasting as an intervention show episode.

Everyone was seated around a large conference table. One by one, each person was allowed the opportunity to speak about my progress or to ask questions about my current and future care. The purpose of this meeting was to get my family and me ready for the next step, which was discharge and the decisions we would need to make. So much was involved in my care, and I was not prepared for what we were about to hear. The thought of it scared me to my core. So much information to process packed into about an hour was overwhelming for me. Up to this point, I was going along with the program. Going home was not something that had entered my mind. It was the farthest thing from my mind. I was overwhelmed with my paralysis and the many unknowns of what was to come.

The meeting started with the facilitator's statement, "Thank you all for coming and we appreciate your presence here today. We are here to talk about the progress, concerns, and future needs for John Chartier. Our ultimate goal is to help ensure that John has a successful transition from MetroHealth to home or any other facility. We will start with the staff and continue around the table, but feel free to ask questions when appropriate."

My nurse, Angela, and the head of nursing started with the formalities, and then they went right to the heart of their observations about me. It had been a week since my feeding tube was removed, and Angela noticed that my appetite had increased since solid foods were added to my diet. The hospital's food was very bland and unappetizing. The truth was my appetite changed because food from outside the hospital was being brought in from friends and family daily!

She reported that I was having my weight shifted in my wheelchair by changing the seat back and leg angles to relieve pressure points on my body every 15 minutes and that I was being turned in bed from side to side during the night every two hours. There were no pressure sores on my body, and she intended to keep it that way. Coming to MetroHealth, I had a shearing bedsore on my tailbone, which was always a concern. I did go on to have pressure sores on my feet from the shoes rubbing them, but I couldn't feel it.

The report was unbelievably detailed regarding my daily routine and extremely specific about what would be needed after discharge. The head of nursing took over to stress I needed to be in charge of my care and advocate for myself. She continued telling us that after I would leave the hospital, there would be many challenges in the future.

My physical therapist (PT) and occupational therapist (OT) were the next to report. They talked about my progress since arrival. Not much. It was still too early. All the therapy was geared toward functional goals and keeping my body moving. They were keeping my arms in motion to stay away from contracture. Contracture is a condition of shortening and hardening of muscles, tendons, or other tissue, often leading to deformity and joint rigidity. This would hinder any fluid motion I would need in therapy. The occupational therapists used different devices such as a Balanced Forearm Orthosis (BFO) to reteach my arms to move, hoping I may feed myself one day. I needed maximum assistance to be fed, clothed, and cleaned.

The physical therapist spoke about ordering a custom wheelchair that would be fit to my certain specifications. It would need a sip and puff system. (A tube that controls wheelchair movements by blowing or sucking air into the tube). She said it would give me the freedom to drive myself, and it would give me the control of tilting the chair to shift the weight of my body. This was imperative to my body health to reduce the chance of pressure sores. The physical therapy goals were to push me toward balancing, then strengthening for sitting and transferring to my chair before discharge.

These goals all seemed unattainable during the meeting. I had no movement in my arms or hands and minimal function in my legs and feet. The physical therapist spoke of the need for a Hoyer Lift. (A large, expensive lift system to allow others to put me in and lift me out of a wheelchair or bed.) Then updating our home became the next agenda item. A home evaluation was needed to know what modifications were necessary to accommodate my living there. The physical therapist's last item was the need for transportation. We had to consider whether we would get a wheelchair-accessible van or use public transportation. We had many options to consider.

My social worker joined the conversation by asking if we had started applying for Social Security Disability and Medicaid. He told us these two areas are very time-consuming. Applying as quickly as possible would be in our best interest. Rhonda was way out in front of it. She had applied for Social Security Disability on my behalf, and we spoke to a lawyer through a phone conversation. The social worker asked if I would be going home or to a skilled nursing facility. Going home wasn't an option. Rhonda still needed to work, not only for income but also for the health insurance we so desperately relied upon for my care. The meeting left us in shock for all that was still to come. The amount of preparation we would have to do for me to come home seemed insurmountable.

Our family and friends flooded MetroHealth staff with their questions and concerns. My friend, Hope, had the presence of mind, once again, to write down everything that they told us during this meeting. These notes were invaluable to us later as our minds had a hard time remembering the vast amount of information shared that day. It was an informative and overwhelming day for all of us.

I am truly grateful for everyone in the room that day, knowing they took time to care about my future and how they could help. It was a time of such great emotion that welled up inside me as I sat there and listened. So much uncertainty, yet there was a collective group of individuals discussing my every possible need and how those needs could be met.

It was so early in my process at MetroHealth, and it sounded like they were pushing for me to go home. It was expressed to me that most individuals typically stay an average of 2 to 4 weeks. This information helped me to understand they were not rushing me to go home but instead explaining the reality of health insurance companies. The big difference for me was that I had an insurance advocate named Connie, who was trying everything to help me get a longer stay at the rehab hospital. As this entire process unfolded, my advocate extended my stay for three months, which was almost an unheard-of feat. As my case manager, Connie was a bulldog! She tried to get me anything and everything that she thought would be helpful for my progress. I am still in awe.

CHAPTER 11

How I Became the Mayor of Metro

My support team empowered me to become strong enough to be part of the bigger team of patients at MetroHealth. Losing mobility and hearing the words quadriplegic can quickly take away your sense of identity. It meant a great deal the first time someone called me the Mayor of Metro. As silly as that may sound, this nickname given represented the formation of my newly expanded identity. When you face reevaluating your life, you learn to pay close attention to what has meaning for you and the people around you. I realized that I was still myself, I had value, and that my sense of self was expanded, not reduced.

When I understood that my purpose at MetroHealth was to bring humor or just have a conversation with others, I was inspired to reach out and make people smile. I love making people laugh, and soon a fire was ignited within me. I had always tried to be a helpful person, but now I did not have to try. I felt joy in helping. It became my passion, and that passion has endured and evolved to this day.

At first, when you process the level of your injury, it seems there will never be anything to laugh or be happy about again in your life. I do not exactly know what day it was that I saw the humor in life again, but I know it was following Rhonda's words that she was not leaving me. She made me laugh that day, and I knew I did not want to fall apart into a dark, deep pit of despair. I knew how close I was to that pit, so I tried to help my fellow patients see some humor in their lives as well. I knew giving them a spark could make a huge difference. It certainly did for me.

I remember a Saturday morning when my arms and legs were not working yet. Rhonda had not arrived, and the staff had put me in my wheelchair for the day. At this time, I had no control of any kind, so I could not manipulate a wheelchair. I depended on others to put me in it, move me around, and take me out of it. The head nurse came into my room and told me they were doing crafts in the main hospitality room. She said that the staff had gathered rocks to decorate with paint and nail polish. They wanted me to come out of my room and participate, and I said, "No way." I thought it was a ridiculous request since I did not have the ability for that type of activity. My mind did not grasp the big picture of why she wanted me to participate. In retrospect, it was about being with others who had diminished abilities. It was about community.

About five minutes later, the head nurse came in, and she said jokingly, "John, I am going to paint your fingernails, and there is nothing you can do about it." She and I had such a great rapport, so I said she could paint them, which surprised her. She asked me what color I wanted them painted, so I replied, "Yellow and blue, of course." When she came back to my room with the polish and a big smile on her face, she wanted to know which finger I wanted to be yellow and which one to be blue. Again, I surprised her by saying, "Paint all my nails and alternate between blue and yellow on each finger."

In disbelief, she exclaimed, "Really?"

I replied emphatically, "Absolutely!"

It was hilarious because I was in a hospital in Ohio, and I am a huge Michigan fan, but nobody knew it. To put this in perspective, the University of Michigan school colors are yellow (Maize) and blue. She did as I asked, and she finished right before Rhonda arrived. As Rhonda entered my hospital room, my wheelchair was facing the doorway, my arms and hands were on the armrests. With an instant smile, she blurted out, "What happened to your fingernails?" After my brief explanation, Rhonda and I had a good laugh about my fingernails, knowing I had pulled one over (a joke) on the nurse. It was so encouraging to hear her laugh.

Interestingly, Rhonda had brought me a blanket from home that day because it was always cold in the hospital, and it was a University of Michigan blanket. The school colors and inscription were unmistakable. The timing was perfect. Rhonda wrapped it around me and wheeled me out into the hospitality/common room.

When my nurse saw me, she laughed so hard, realizing I had tricked her. She had no idea I was a Michigan fan. Her initial surprise that I would let her paint my nails now made sense. She laughed hysterically, knowing I went from not doing crafts to tricking her into painting my nails the colors of Ohio State's biggest rival. I believe she was expecting that everyone on the floor was probably an Ohio State fan. She certainly was. It was great. It was a moment of normal, fun human interaction. After all these horrible weeks, finally, laughing seemed normal. It felt good.

As the days became months, I constantly looked for ways to encourage and uplift people. Another example of this happened on the morning of my birthday when one of the nurses came into my room to give me birthday greetings and promptly placed a sparkly tiara on my shiny bald head. I'm sure most people hospitalized under such catastrophic circumstances would not have appreciated that gesture, but this was an opportunity for me to bring a little levity to this day. This amused the nurses so much that many asked to take my picture. We were all taken in by this funny moment, letting the harsh reality subside.

Immediately after, I drove my wheelchair from room to room, saying good morning and chatting with other patients if they wanted. There were many laughs and engaging conversations as to why I had a tiara on my head. Exactly what I was hoping for.

This opportunity led the staff to ask me if I would visit fellow patients on the floor whenever they saw the need for encouragement. It was very humbling to be asked, but on the other hand, it was very uplifting having those personal interactions for them and myself.

I think that passion for encouraging and uplifting others continued to grow not only for those who surrounded me but to keep me grounded and engaged. The patients and staff on my floor became important to me. My Spinal Cord Injury (SCI) family continues to provide richness to my life I did not expect.

Together, we share heartache and victory. Our injuries range from complete paralysis to partial paralysis, and our levels of recovery are individual. It is painful and encouraging to watch your friends fight for every level of function. The friends I have made through this process have given me so much enrichment to my life, and they are an enormous part of my story. Almost every day in occupational therapy a topic would start a comical discussion, such as a TV show called, *The Bachelor*. I had never watched it, but the therapists spoke about it with so much passion, I couldn't resist joining in with some chiding or acting like it was the greatest show ever made. I had no clue, but this made for some fun times.

My time in physical therapy with Amanda was just as entertaining but more so talking about my favorite subject, baseball. I know she loved the conversations as much as I did because of her passion for the game. The interactions we had each day in therapy and on the floor, I feel, have bonded us forever. Because of these interactions and my passion to be an encouragement to others, somehow this gave someone the funny idea to give me the nickname, 'The Mayor of Metro."

"The power is about waking up every day and making a difference in somebody else's life."
– Nashville Mayor, Megan Barry

One of my goals regarding encouraging my fellow patients was to help them to see, as I now saw, that their value did not change because of their injury. They were still there. Nothing had changed on the inside.

I found an analogy to illustrate this point I now use when I do public speaking, especially at schools. I will start my talk by holding up a brand-new dollar bill, and I will ask the audience, "Who would like to have this dollar bill?" Generally, the entire audience will raise their hands. I then crumple up the dollar bill and again ask them, "Who wants this dollar bill now?" Again, all hands are raised. I will then put the dollar bill on the ground and stomp on it, grinding it with my shoe onto the floor, getting it dirty, and ask them again, "Who wants the dollar bill now?" All hands are again raised. At that point, I will talk to the audience about realizing that the dollar bill value remains the same, whether it is pristine and new, crumpled up or crumpled up and dirty. The value does not change.

I then tell them that people are the same. When we are completely healthy and able-bodied, we are of the same value as we are with a disability. Our inherent value is the same. That message is the vital message I wanted my fellow survivors to understand because it was a message that my heart deeply needed to hear. When I understood that truth, everything changed. When I realized that my value was unchanged from my accident, I dared to live and evolve. And as the Mayor of Metro, I wanted each of my fellow patients to realize they were equally valuable.

During my three months at MetroHealth, I made incredible physical and emotional gains. I went from only being able to move my eyes and lips to the excitement of moving a toe, eventually my foot, then my second foot, my legs, and then my right hand, all within three months. The movements were minimal at first, but with the movement came hope. Every day I worked many hours with my therapists to gain more movement and function. We never knew when my progress would slow down, so each newly regained function was monumental.

Each movement came back slowly, such as getting me to sit on the edge of a mat table. I lost the abilities of movement and balance, but with many days and weeks of practicing, I regained some of that function. There was failure after failure, but our persistence (mine and the therapist, Amanda) paid off. This brought back memories of my childhood, trying to learn how to ride a bicycle. I saw other friends riding bicycles. It looked so easy to do, and I wanted to learn, but attempt after attempt, I would fall. I would put all my might into every movement, much like trying to sit upon the mat table only to have the same results of trying to balance on the bicycle. Each failed attempt with the bicycle and mat table made me push myself harder. My physical therapist, Amanda, tracked my time by how long I could stay balanced. Five seconds, twenty seconds, forty seconds, and so on. Although I felt the excitement as my balancing time kept increasing each day, I also felt the frustration of not balancing as easily as I did before. I am grateful for Amanda, with her knowledge, persistence, and caring, which ignited my desire to keep pushing through.

After many weeks of trying to master the sit and balance, we added the hardest challenge I would face. STANDING! This proved to be difficult, considering the pushback from my body. This process consumed my physical therapy time. It started with a test, initially being strapped onto a standing table. From the parallel lying position, the table was slowly tilted, vertical being the goal. I discovered within a matter of 30 seconds why the table is tilted slowly. As Amanda tilted me on the table, she watched intently to see my reaction. And then it happened. With the table at a thirty-degree angle, I drifted into unconsciousness. The test was finished for the day. Blood pressure came into play again for me.

According to SpinalCord.com, "The spinal cord is an integral part of the body's central nervous system (CNS). In addition to serving as the communication conduit for the body and brain, it is also responsible for regulating blood pressure in the body. When the spinal cord is injured, the body may not be able to regulate or maintain the appropriate blood pressure, either increasing or decreasing to dangerous levels." This led to many times of unconsciousness for me. You may have had this happen when you stand up too fast and get dizzy. Well, that is exactly what it was like, but I would pass out or faint.

There was a morning routine the staff equipped me with to help combat the blood pressure drop. Items like an abdominal binder attached to my midsection, Ace elastic wraps from my thighs down to my feet or compression hose. It certainly was an adventure getting me out of bed and ready for therapy. All I could do was sit there and look pretty.

Sometime later, Amanda decided we would skip the standing table and go directly to standing from my wheelchair. I said aloud, "No way!" Amanda assured me I would not fall. Trust was so important. She had gained my trust. First, a gait belt (a belt device, typically four inches wide, put on a patient with mobility issues) was strapped to my waist, and then I was coached as to what she wanted me to do. There were three therapists, one at each arm and one standing in front of me, ready to grab the gait belt. I was told all my energy needed to be pushed into my legs as they helped me up. Amanda counted, one, two, three. They pulled, and I started to rise, and everything went black. I woke up back sitting in my wheelchair as a blood pressure cuff was being put onto my arm. I expected this to happen each time I was helped to stand.

After a week of failed attempts, aided by two physical therapists and my arms strapped on a platform walker. My description of a platform walker would give you, the reader, a picture of Frankenstein walking with arms straight forward and parallel to the ground. A person without much hand strength can find using a walker to be difficult, since they have a hard time gripping the walker and using their hands to bear weight. A platform walker with wheels allows the user to put weight on their forearms (area between wrist and elbow) instead of on their hands. I was able to stand up and take a step. It felt like a miracle. I cannot put into words the elation that flowed through my inner self for each movement I achieved.

With each passing day, I knew that I would soon have to leave MetroHealth. Our health insurance would decide based upon how many days they would approve of my stay on an assessment of my needs and my progress. I had watched many of my new friends be released from the hospital's care, so it was on my mind quite often. I knew I needed more therapy, but I also wanted to go home. This was like the game tug of war. Unfortunately, this game was being played out in my mind. The tugging of therapy with the possibility of more gains and the pulling of my heartstrings to being at home.

I anticipated the day when I would get a day pass for a visit to my house. The sole purpose of a day pass was to get patients back out into the world and experience what we may expect once we leave the hospital. In addition, it was to find out what you may experience and how to adjust and cope with the hurdles you may face when you leave the hospital, going into your home and community. I must admit it was both exciting and unnerving at the same time.

After much time had passed, I was stable enough to travel and given the opportunity to go home for a day pass. My desire to be in my own home was an urgent and intense need. I really missed being home. I missed our two dogs (Maize and Blue), the taste of Rhonda's cooking. When the day arrived, my transport driver was an hour and a half late to pick me up, which cut my time at home down by that amount. I felt very frustrated because my longing for being at home was so great. The transport driver came to my room and led me outside the hospital, where a tall, long van was parked. She opened the back double doors, grabbed a controller and lowered a platform to the ground. She asked me to drive my wheelchair onto the platform to lift and load me and the chair into the van.

As the platform rose, my sense of feeling in space once again did not fit the circumstance. My heart was racing and pounding in my chest. It felt as though I were as high as a one-story building and was about to topple off it. Once inside, she locked my wheelchair to the floor with ratchet straps. It wasn't until that moment, I felt secure. My driver asked me the question of what had happened to me as she drove toward home. I responded with my personal story but not in great detail. When I had finished speaking, her reply was, "I am sorry to hear that." She turned on the radio, and the conversation was over. My anticipation of going home and no more conversation made my perception of the trip seem like many hours had passed rather than the fifty-five minutes it actually took.

When we arrived home, in my wheelchair, I was lowered out of the van onto the driveway where my wife Rhonda, my daughter Jordyn, and my dogs greeted me. I was so excited to be there with them as my emotions overwhelmed me. After the hugs from Rhonda, Jordyn, and the dogs, a question popped into my mind. How will I get into the house? I did not see a ramp for my wheelchair. Rhonda opened the garage door to reveal that my friends and father-in-law had built me an entrance into the house with a lift for my wheelchair. I was told that Sue, my supervisor at Chrysler, had paid for the lift. I was astonished by the giving of money, time, kindness, and love that was done so I had a way into my home. It was another humbling moment in my life.

When I made my way into the house, it was like I was seeing everything for the first time. There was this beautiful feeling I was experiencing, much like how I felt hugging my newly born children. At that moment, it was like how a newborn must feel being wrapped in a blanket, the embrace of a warm hug, love, and security. As I sat in my wheelchair in the middle of our living room, I could smell pleasant aromas wafting from the kitchen. Rhonda had made this wonderful meal that seemed like a distant memory. It was amazing to eat it in my own home! Of course, I could not feed myself, but Rhonda made sure I had enough to eat. Everything felt new. I did not want to leave. For such a brief amount of time at home, almost everything seemed right in my world.

At the end of my day pass visit, the transport driver arrived fifteen minutes early, cutting into my time—again. What an emotional rollercoaster. I went from extreme excitement to such sadness I had to leave. My heart was crushed thinking about going back. I remember telling Rhonda I just wanted to stay there even though we both knew it was not feasible. Getting loaded into the van was so somber. The driver navigated me and my wheelchair onto the transport lift into the van and strapped me securely. As she started up the van Rhonda, Jordyn, and the dogs stood there watching. I felt devastated.

After maneuvering the transport van to the end of the driveway, my new driver stopped to type in the address on the GPS unit to MetroHealth, and the first words out of her mouth were, "Oh my goodness, I have heard all about you. I heard you have an amazing story to tell, and I want to hear everything. Don't leave anything out!" Talk about being taken by surprise! She was not the same driver who brought me home. I would say she was completely the opposite in terms of personality.

As we drove away from the house, I told her my story, and she kept saying, "Wow, that is a God moment." She totally got it. She was like a sponge, absorbing everything I said. When I was done with my story, I could see her eyes in the rearview mirror from my vantage point. She had tears streaming down her face, and I could hear the change of emotion in her voice. She told me that my story was amazing and inspiring. I could tell by her response she was a spiritual person, so I asked her to tell me her story.

She said, "I don't have a story."

I chuckled and told her that everyone has a story! Again, her eyes met mine in the rearview mirror.

"Well," she said, "I guess I do have a little bit of a story that I will share with you."

She told me that she was expanding her thoughts about her spiritual beliefs, and it was causing a rift with her husband. One night she had a dream and said it felt so real. God appeared before her and said to go out and spread His Word. She continued, "I was so taken aback because, at the beginning of the dream, I was drowning, and God pulled me out of the water and saved me. It was then God told me to spread His Word: 'Tell others about me and what I did for you.'"

She continued, "When I awoke that morning, I told my husband about my dream and how I had believed it. He told me I was a crazy woman and to stop the nonsense. I told him I was doing it with or without him because he did not believe in this God or my dream. From that moment, he became verbally abusive. The verbal abuse continued until I could not take any more. I contemplated my options. Not wanting my children or myself to be subjected to this abuse any longer, I took my kids and left him. For me, to do this is a big deal as a foreign person in this country. I am now going to school for biblical studies and raising my two kids by myself. I feel that God led me to this job, to be a transport driver so I could meet you. Maybe it was to hear your and other inspirational stories."

I had no idea that mine was an inspirational story.

I have heard many stories in my life, but her story was very compelling. I could not believe she was somewhat reluctantly sharing this with me. She was sincere in her words and demeanor, sharing she felt God led her to be a transport driver, maybe to hear my story. It was a very emotional day.

When we arrived at MetroHealth, she took me and my wheelchair out of the transport van and gave me a small book of daily devotionals. She removed a small baseball bat and ball that dangled from her keychain. Looking at me, shrugging her shoulders, she smiled and said, "I don't know if you like baseball, but I would like you to have this." She put the baseball bat and ball keychain into the devotional book as a bookmark. She said it had been on her keychain for a few years and was given to her as a keepsake. Smiling and chuckling, she said, "I really don't know why I have kept this on my keychain these past years. It always seems to get in my way. I believe you are the reason." What a sweet and kind gesture. She could never comprehend the feelings I have about baseball and how it helped me survive my turbulent childhood. What may seem like a simple gift to most was a noticeably big deal to me at that very moment.

Her story and her gift filled me with a renewed strength after the crushing frustration of having to leave my home and return to the hospital. Her leap of faith was incredible. She floated in and out of my life exactly when I needed to be reminded of God's love and support in every moment, no matter how disheartened I was feeling. It amazed me she was led to give me a baseball bat and ball! How did she know of my love of baseball? There are coincidences in life that you can shrug off, but this interaction was so vastly different to me. Truly there are an infinite number of things we can believe in, but I never saw her again. I believe that our paths crossed for both of our benefits.

When fear crept into my heart, I held on tightly to the feeling of God's presence from that day. Getting my pass to go home meant I was getting close to discharge, and I was dreading leaving one of the top spinal cord trauma centers in the country for an unknown facility.

The closer I came to discharge, the more I worried about how horrible it would be. A few of my fellow patients told me stories of what I could encounter when going to a step-down facility, and that concerned me. To prepare me, the staff at MetroHealth repeatedly told me, "As you leave this hospital, be your own advocate." They said it over and over and over until it stuck in my head, causing me some anxiety. Why did I need to be my own advocate? I had had a few surgeries in the past, a tonsillectomy, an appendectomy, several sports-related injury repairs, and my heart valve replacement. It had never occurred to me that I needed to be my own advocate. I always assumed that medical professionals would do the best thing for me. I had not considered that every patient is an individual and may have specific and personalized needs. This was the first time I understood the importance of self-advocacy in a medical setting. I was leaving a secure environment where I had trusted the staff to take care of my every need, and now I was going into the unknown, and I needed to fight for my own health needs truly. I felt great distress.

One person who helped me at this time was Herb. Herb was the president of the spinal cord chapter of Northeast Ohio and a volunteer at MetroHealth. He spent a lot of time on the spinal cord floor and in the therapy department. I felt as though he was my mentor, and he gave me insight into what life on the outside of the hospital would be like living in a wheelchair. Herb was both very personable and likable, which cemented our new friendship. He was always encouraging and would be open and honest with me about how difficult situations could be. He told me it was okay to feel vulnerable because we all do at times. Herb has definitely been a positive example of what a person can accomplish as a volunteer, which has been powerful in my recovery.

At the end of June, I knew my discharge was imminent. My, insurance advocate, Connie, had already secured for me more days of treatment than most of the patients on the unit were able to get. I was grateful to her. I knew she could not get me much more time at MetroHealth.

When I received the news that my discharge date was July 5th, I was not surprised. July 4th, 2013, was my last night at MetroHealth. It was a special night for me. Rhonda and I had dinner together, and she stayed until 7:00 pm, knowing she would be returning in the morning for my discharge. The staff planned to show a movie in the common room for anyone on the Spinal Cord Injury floor to watch. I still had friends on the unit, and we watched a movie and ate popcorn until the city of Cleveland fireworks started. On the spinal cord floor at MetroHealth, much of the building is surrounded by solid glass windows. It's because of this, we saw the fireworks very clearly. We watched as city after city along Lake Erie set off their fireworks display. It was a wow moment of connection for us as friends and patients. We had no idea there would be so many cities along the lake having firework displays. It was spectacular.

The excitement of the night was in direct contrast with the dread I felt the next morning. The dread was mainly because of the unknown of my next facility. I presumed this change would be horrible. Teary-eyed, I said goodbye to all the staff and my new friends. Spending more than three months with this staff and now leaving them behind was difficult because they became like family. They were part of my identity. As I waited for my transport to arrive, I could not stop my emotions. Losing security and friendship was more than I could tolerate. It was a sad day indeed.

CHAPTER 12

The Post-Acute Rehabilitation Facility

"There comes a time when you have to choose between turning the page and closing the book."

—Josh Jameson

As I look back over this period of my life, I realize this was one of the most impactful moments in my journey. I had to decide to turn the page, leave my comfort, and go into the post-acute rehab facility without any security that they would know how to care for me. I had to take a leap of faith that I could find my way, and it was very unsettling, and I did not feel comfortable with those emotions. I am a normal guy (at least I think I am) who does not enjoy having an emotional outburst in front of people, so my emotions turned to internal frustration when my transport driver was late. The pick-up was scheduled to arrive around noon, but that did not happen. A hospital administrator told us she would look into why there was such a delay.

There I sat in my wheelchair, feeling miserable. I kept thinking, "Let's get this over with so I can stop feeling such sadness." The driver finally arrived at 3:20 pm, signed some documents, and loaded me into the transport van. As we pulled away from MetroHealth, I felt ungrounded. The waiting had increased my anxiety, and to make matters worse, the driver was unsure of where he was taking me. He had a general idea, but I had to direct him as he made a couple of wrong turns. It was disorienting to try to give directions after being inside a facility for so long and not driving, but it was obvious this driver needed help. The hour in the van was unsettling and increased my frustration. Okay, maybe I was really annoyed!

When we finally arrived at the post-acute rehabilitation facility, I was unloaded from the transport van and was ready for the transition to begin. Rhonda had met us there, and I maneuvered my power wheelchair through the doors. It was not at all what I had expected. The facility was beautiful! I thought, "This is starting well." A staff member who greeted us immediately gave many important instructions and took us to the room I would now call home. I was then helped to transfer into my hospital bed that was a bit too short for my tall frame. We were told that maintenance would be called to bring me a longer bed. We were shown my personal bathroom with an emergency pull chain and the room climate controls. That was not something I could do for myself. The last instruction was to press the red button on a handheld device clipped to the bed rail if I needed assistance. WHAT? How would I press a button? I did not have the function in my arms or hands to feasibly attain that goal. Although they insisted they could meet my needs, it quickly became clear that they had never taken care of someone with a spinal cord injury. I was told to press a button if I needed someone to come, but that was physically impossible for me to do. I explained that I could not press a button because my arms and hands would not allow for this precise function.

Before this, Rhonda visited and called multiple rehab facilities to find care for me close to our home. Some came right out and said they could not meet my needs, while others just didn't seem like a good fit for me. Rhonda had been very explicit about my health care requirements when she spoke to the facility head about whether they could meet those needs. She was assured that it would not be a problem, and everything would be ready for my arrival. Now I worried there would be no way for me to call for help. At MetroHealth hospital, I used a sip and puff device where I blew into a straw, and that lit up a nursing station light so someone would know I needed assistance. I was also remarkably close to a nursing station, so I didn't feel far from any aid that I might need. Here I was tucked away into a corner, far from a nurse's station, where no one would hear me if I called for assistance. I felt helpless. My worst fear was already happening, not being able to get help.

As if not being able to call for help was not enough stress, I immediately had another dilemma. When I told them I needed to be turned every two hours since this was not possible for me to do myself, several nursing assistants told me that would not happen for me, especially since they were not given instructions to do so. I knew I had to be rotated or I would develop pressure sores. I knew how critical turning while lying in bed was to my health, so I asked for Human Resources to come into my room and have that conversation. I had to plead my case. I did not need a pressure wound on top of everything else that I had to manage. They made it happen once they understood. A longer bed arrived later in the day equipped with an alternating pressure mattress, and a unique call button was ordered. I had a quick lesson in what it meant to be my own advocate. The words from MetroHealth, "Be your own advocate," flooded back and echoed in my brain.

Although the staff was excellent, they did not have experience with spinal cord injuries as I expected. As I shared my prior treatment and expectations, they quickly told me that my care would differ from what I had experienced at MetroHealth. This was not the beginning I had hoped for at my new facility. My transition started rough because I expected them to understand what I had been through over the past three and a half months, but they had no frame of reference. They had not had a patient dealing with the issues I had. Once I pushed for what I needed, the staff made great efforts to help me. They always wanted to help, but they did not understand my injuries when I arrived. As my stay continued, we learned to work together, and I forged ahead to make progress. The staff worked diligently to learn about my specific needs and help me recover, and it did not take long for one of my major issues, spasms, to give us all plenty of opportunity to learn.

Spasms are among the many issues involved with a spinal cord injury, and they can be extremely painful. A spasm is similar to a charley horse in your thigh or calf, but mine was full body and could last for hours, which is the extreme. Often, they would grip me, let go, and then grip me again in just a few seconds. If you walked in on me experiencing spasms, it would appear that I was having a seizure, except that I am fully conscious and in extreme pain that I cannot control in any way. I can spasm myself right out of my wheelchair or off my bed. I can't control it at all! To relieve my whole-body spasms, the only relief has been sedation. This type of medication releases the muscle spasms and puts me to sleep for hours which causes other issues such as loss of control of the bladder and bowels. It really is a careful balance of sedation. Too much sedation can stop your breathing.

One morning my nursing assistant came in to get my weight and help me to get ready for the day. Within a few minutes of her arrival, I went into spasms. She immediately called for a nurse and stayed with me as I was writhing in pain. She sat on the edge of my bed, holding my hand until my nurse could come and give me the protocol of medication. They both stayed with me, giving me words of encouragement until the medication kicked in and the spasms released. I eventually drifted to sleep. Because of the spasms, they canceled my physical therapy for the day, but Kevin, my physical therapist, still came to my room. I still awoke to much discomfort.

Kevin took his job very seriously and wanted to help in any way that he could. Although I did not leave my bed, Kevin decided he might be able to calm my symptoms and performed a procedure called rhythmic rotation on each limb. This is a therapy to release muscle tension in the body with no exertion from the patient. It seemed to really help my body relax. Even my occupational therapist stopped in at the end of her day to check on me. Each professional went above and beyond their job requirements to help me. I was grateful for many similar incidences, where the dedicated professionals at the facility helped me in my recovery. My trust grew through experiencing their care, which helped me be comfortable and engaged with them.

Sometime after the accident, while at MetroHealth, I developed a craving for sweet things. This was very unusual for me, but this craving followed me to the post-acute rehab facility. I asked Rhonda to buy me a large assortment of candy. I had a whole dresser drawer dedicated to it. I told everyone who came to my room to help themselves because it was there for me to share. I loved to see the joy a piece of chocolate or hard candy would bring to a person's face.

I was about twenty years younger than most of the other patients, so my room soon became the hangout with staff often stopping to talk to me. Also, because I was younger, I would stay up later than most patients. Although many came in to talk, I wanted to believe it was not just for the candy. I felt human, like a person as well as a patient. I tried hard to maintain my positive attitude from MetroHealth and encouraged both the staff and the patients. I quickly realized that everything in my life is about attitude. I worked hard mentally to stay optimistic and thankful for each day. I noticed how important it was for the professionals working with me to be positive. They definitely set the tone for the patients, and I was grateful to have like-minded people working with me.

Being part of this community helped me focus on my goals for myself, and I soon began to share my goals with the professionals working with me. When I wheeled myself with the powerchair into the post-acute rehab facility for the first time, I said to Rhonda, "I will walk out of here." I did not know then that I would spend seven and a half months in this facility, but I did know I had a goal I intended to reach. That goal was my daily focus. I did not know if my injury would allow my body to have that kind of recovery, but that did not stop my focus. I needed rest, and I needed therapy. I needed someone to push me to my limits.

For the first two weeks of therapy, I had two physical therapists. They were both pleasant individuals, and their therapy methods were fine, but I didn't like being switched back and forth every few days. I guess it was the team's words at MetroHealth instructing me to direct my own care that emboldened me to ask for the same therapist each day. I also asked for someone who would challenge me. I had heard they would provide therapy on Saturdays for special circumstances, so I asked for that. The therapy manager reluctantly agreed, assigning me to a guy named Kevin and granting me Saturday therapy.

Kevin and I meshed right from the start. He was different in a good way. Instead of reading my file and jumping right into therapy on our first day, we talked for a while. We discussed my ultimate goal and the process forward in reaching that objective. Having had some progress at MetroHealth, walking one day again was always on my mind. He regularly evaluated me to see what I could or could not do, and then we would talk about how to proceed.

Kevin always had conversations with me when he knew I was not ready to push forward, but he had the discernment to know when I was actually ready. He would research spinal cord injuries at home and come in with a new game plan for me. I respected his commitment to learn about spinal cord injuries to help me in my recovery. We had so much in common it made working with him something I looked forward to each day. Therapy became a highlight of my day instead of a grind where you hate to go. It was a definite challenge, not just for me, it was for Kevin. As time went on, I could tell from our interactions I was more than just another patient. Kevin and I developed a friendship, one we keep to this day.

Over the next seven-plus months, I developed relationships,

and a new sense of family emerged for me there. My goal became their goal. I will always be grateful to the staff for working so hard with me to regain mobility and strength, and I appreciate their efforts to help me attain my goal. With Rhonda's help holding my hand, I did walk out of there in February of 2014, a little more than eleven months after my accident. Before my injury, walking was much like breathing. You take in breaths of air without thinking about doing it. Breathing just happens. Walking was similar, I didn't have to think about it. In the past, I would walk toward my destination without really thinking about each step. The movement just happened. Today it is much different. Each step is thought out and very deliberate. I have to think about each step and visually see it happen.

I have often thought, "Why me?" Not why did this happen to me, but why am I able to walk when so many of my new friends cannot walk. I cannot deny the ability to walk is incredible. However, it took intense work from my family and me to get to this level of recovery. I know each injury is completely different, and so are the outcomes. The difference between the potential for recovery comes down to a difference in the injury. One person's injury can be so similar to another, but a minuscule difference can totally affect the severity of the injury and the outcome. Factors such as rapid response and skill of the emergency medical technicians, hospital intake care, surgeons and therapists' expertise all contribute to physical recovery. Still, they do not help with the guilt of recovery. I have read and listened to speakers talk about survivor guilt and understand the concept. I feel I've been living with a form of this that I am calling recovery guilt. I do live with many issues due to my spinal cord injury that have taken away many of my abilities to do some of the simplest of tasks. However, standing and taking steps is something that many individuals who have suffered a spinal cord injury cannot perform. I live with this huge weight on my heart every day. It is very humbling, and I try never to take anything for granted.

"Everybody has a story. And there's something to be learned from every experience."

– Oprah Winfrey

I have many great stories from my time in the post-acute rehab facility, but one of my favorites shows the staff's spirit and how we bonded. I was a big fan of gummy bears, Haribo brand, and always had a large stash of them in a drawer. It was late one evening, and I was watching TV and eating some gummy bears. I accidentally dropped one, and it fell to the floor. With no sensation of gripping objects in my hands, this was a common occurrence for me. I completely forgot to tell my nursing assistant before I went to sleep for the night I had dropped a gummy bear. It was one of those translucent gummies, and with the type of tile on the floor of my room, it was hard to spot. The next day housekeeping came in to clean my room. She was a wonderful woman named Ramona. Ramona loved to share her own candy stashed away on her cart. She was always pleasant and engaging in conversation, sometimes sharing some of her life stories, talking as she cleaned. We had so many laughs. I cannot describe how she brightened my day just from our conversations.

It wasn't until after Ramona was done mopping and had left the room that my thoughts came back to the lone gummy bear that fell to the floor the last evening. I scoured the room with my eyes and could not see it. It was gone, or so I thought. It was later that day my eyes spotted it, barely! The next day the cleaning of my room happened like clockwork. Again, the tiny gummy bear was gone after her mopping but reappeared when it dried. The funny part was it moved and was never in the same spot. I know it may sound ridiculous, but this became my entertainment. This went on for a week. I shared my story with my wife and a nursing assistant. They both wanted to pick it up and throw it away. I begged them not to do it. It stayed. Some days I would not know the fate of my gummy bear until I returned to my room from therapy.

One day that little gummy bear had finally made its way close to the door. I sat in my wheelchair that day and was listening to music and reading when a woman and her dog came into my room for a visit. She worked with the organization that brings in their highly trained dogs to visit patients, hopefully, to brighten their day. I petted the dog because I love dogs and missed my own dogs so much. She told me that she had another dog trained to enter these settings and would visit me the next time it was in the building. I had a great conversation with the owner about her dogs and the things they needed to learn to visit hospitals or

153

rehabilitation facilities. It was time for the two to move onto the next room, so we said our goodbyes with the promise of a return visit. The dog noticed the gummy bear and scooped it up in its mouth on the way out the door. The owner noticed and made him spit it out immediately. These dogs are trained to drop anything from their mouth on the owner's command because it could be a medication that could be harmful. The dog owner picked up the gummy bear and dropped it in the trash. Ugh! Game over! The ironic part of this story—the dog's name was Bear. Laughably, there was a little feeling of disappointment. Fortunately, the story does not end there.

Until this point in time, there were only three people who knew about my gummy bear's movement. This complete story was too funny, and I felt it needed to be shared. As the saying goes, news travels fast, and it did about the demise of my gummy bear. The next day, I was returning to my room after therapy, and when I entered through the doorway, I was greeted with thumb-sized gummy bears everywhere. They were lined up on my headboard, footboard, windowsill, chair, and scattered on my bed. There was a note on my pillow that read, "We know what you did, and we are here for our friend!" I still laugh about that moment and appreciate the nursing assistant who took her own time and spent her own money to brighten my day!

I was always looking for ways to contribute to lightheartedness. I thought I would use the constant information I was given about HIPAA to be a springboard for some fun. The

Health Insurance Portability and Accountability Act of 1996 (HIPAA) is a federal law designed to prevent sensitive patient health information disclosure. The staff had clarified that any HIPAA violation was a serious concern, which made me think about the sign beside the door to my room that said, John Chartier. It hit me that anyone who came down the hall would see John Chartier, violating my privacy, and that seemed like a thing the "HIPAA police" would be all over. I changed the name on my door to Johnny Bravo, a fictitious cartoon character, to be funny and helpful. I thought I was pretty funny until I returned to my room from physical therapy a few days later to find two serious-looking people in my doorway. One of them was Erin, our human resource person, and the other was a state auditor. Erin looked at me and said, "John, what is the meaning of your room name tag being Johnny Bravo instead of John Chartier?" I said, "Well, Erin, we are all about not having HIPAA violations, and I cannot have this facility violating HIPAA!" The state auditor had a smile on her face, and Erin just looked at me before she said, "I will allow it." I loved the hilarious exchange.

A few days later, I was speaking with two nursing assistants in my room, and I heard a voice outside of my room that sounded like my doctor. I heard a few choice words spoken about, where is my patient? It sounded as if he wondered where John Chartier was taken as his voice faded and his footsteps stomped away from my doorway. I knew he was heading back toward the nurse's station. The two nursing assistants did not want to get caught in the crossfire and get the doctor mad, so they took that as their cue it was best to leave my room. I guess the name tag must have thrown him off because a few moments later, my doctor appeared in my doorway.

I'm guessing someone at the nursing desk reassured him that I was still a resident in room 305. He questioned me about the sign outside my door, stating Johnny Bravo resided here. Since the doctor had two young children, I assumed he would know the silliness behind the name. I asked him, "Don't you know who Johnny Bravo is?" He replied, "No!" He was so upset because he thought I was gone from the facility and without his knowledge. I found it to be funny, but he did not!

I honestly looked forward to interactions with my doctor because he was always so serious and did his job well. I enjoyed trying to make him laugh, which also got me laughing as well. That desire fueled my imagination to find other ways to make jokes, and I had many more funny interactions. By the end of my stay, I actually made him laugh, which made my time there just a little more bearable.

Stories like these made preparing to leave the post-acute rehab facility difficult for me. It was a similarly anxious experience as leaving MetroHealth. Frankly, I had become the guy in room 305 with a drawer full of candy and a room always welcoming to staff, patients, and visitors. My room was a place to hang out if you wanted to drop by. This routine was my life every day for over seven months. I had built a community, and I felt safe in the care of the staff. Before being discharged, I was allowed to go home for the day several times, and the visits had always gone fine, but this seemed different. This discharge was permanent. Do not misunderstand, I longed to be at home from the first day this mess happened, but my mind and body felt fragile. I was now heading home with no safety net if something happened. It was time to face my fears, realizing that the work I had done up to this point had prepared me to leave. I would be okay because I had learned to advocate for myself, and I knew what I needed.

On my final day at the post-acute rehab facility, I again said my goodbyes with sadness and gratitude. My final day started just like all the previous days. A nursing assistant woke me up at 6:00 am and helped with my bathroom care, gave me a sponge bath, brushed my teeth, and helped me to get dressed. I was helped back into my wheelchair, and I sat waiting to be weighed before breakfast. Each nursing assistant I encountered said their goodbyes with hugs and well wishes for my future recovery.

As I sat in the wheelchair waiting for my last day of therapy, my mind reflected through my entire stay here at the facility. It was an emotional time. Rhonda signed all the necessary paperwork, and it was time to go home. Scott, a friend of mine, arrived at this time to transport my powerchair and deliver it to my home. I asked him if he would drive it from my room and load it onto his truck because I was about to honor my promise of walking out of the facility. Grabbing Rhonda's hand, I stood from my chair as she helped steady me, looking at each other and smiling. Leaving through the doorway of room 305, I slowly turned around to see the Johnny Bravo placard one more time. We made the painfully slow trek through the hallways towards the front doors, with me awkwardly stumbling a couple of times, passing many staff who extended their well wishes. As we made it to the foyer at the front of the building, standing there were many of the staff applauding and cheering. My senses were so heightened from the chatter. It was as if this was the World Series, and I was on the winning team. What an incredible moment of excitement. Some of the staff helped load me and my belongings in our vehicle and we set off for home. The story played out as it did in my head a little more than seven months prior. Turning the page on my inpatient treatment, I began a new chapter in the story of rebuilding my life.

CHAPTER 13
Coming Home

"The thrill of coming home has never changed."

—Guy Pearce

How can I describe what it felt like getting into our vehicle? Leaving was painful and exhilarating at the same time, and I could hardly wait to pull into our driveway. I was so emotional. As I came through the door, I was overwhelmed with the feeling of home. It was warm. It was love. It was joy. This was IT. It was intangible, yet a physical sensation as real as the floor and the walls. Finally, after 11 months, it was the feeling of home.

How do you express the emotion of getting back something you've lost? Rarely do we appreciate what we have until we lose it. I didn't know what home was until I lost it. Even though there were huge challenges, coming home gave me back the sense of who I was before my injury and who I continued to be.

My transition was helped immensely by three nursing assistants from the rehab facility, Charissa, Sarah, and Stefanie, who were willing to work for Rhonda and me at our home in addition to their regular jobs at the facility. I could not be left home alone and that frustrated me. I had regained a great deal of function but not the amount I needed to take care of myself properly or safely.

Having these ladies work in our home gave Rhonda peace of mind that I would be cared for while she was working during the day. Their care provided a way for us to get through the remainder of the school year until Rhonda was off for summer break. I cannot imagine how difficult it would have been without them. They were instrumental in my daily care besides taking me to outpatient therapy outside our home. We needed that help to fill the gap for my care from February through June of 2014. Their care allowed Rhonda to keep her teaching position, which was particularly important to us financially and critical to her professionally. She is an excellent teacher and enjoys being in the classroom, and I didn't want her to lose the career she loves.

We also had a lot of help from family and friends as we negotiated the new outpatient therapy schedule, especially the help from my father-in-law, Ted. Asking for help in this regard can be very humbling. I needed the help but thought this would be an enormous burden because of the long-term commitment. Neither Ted nor anyone else ever gave me the impression that I was a burden, but I still sometimes felt that way. Whenever I asked Ted to take me, he always said yes and continually carted me to therapy two to three times a week for the next two years.

This was an enormous time commitment of 45 minutes round trip and waiting at least two hours while I worked at therapy. He never wanted compensation in return, always helping me with a smile on his face. I'm sure there were days he didn't feel up to the task, but he did it anyway. My father-in-law is a shining example of how I, too, want to be — always helping others when they are in need.

And so, it began, the next step in my incredibly long road of therapy. I chose our regional hospital outpatient therapy program because it was close to home, had many therapists and aquatic therapy. My first day was the intake and evaluation process. They needed to get a baseline on my abilities or lack thereof, and I needed to see the facility's offerings, including the equipment, the therapists, and the pool. We were given a starting schedule and an introduction to Scott, the occupational therapist, Barry, the pool therapist, and Andrea, the physical therapist. I was eager to get started.

On my first day of therapy with Andrea, I walked in with my walker. I had my first session with her that lasted roughly a little more than an hour. As I started to leave, she stopped me by asking if I could walk without using a walker. I told her, yes, but not well. This prompted her to ask if I had a cane. I told her I did, only using it sparingly at home and she said, "Great!" Andrea brought me a cane to try out and asked me to walk with it. She watched and I did as she asked. It was within a few moments she stopped me and said, "Don't bring the walker anymore because we will be using your cane."

I was surprised, but I think she was evaluating if I would push myself right from the start. Her approach was to evaluate my baseline function level, and every day she would add a little bit of a challenge to see if I could handle it, which was great for me. From the start, I knew she had the perfect personality to mesh with mine. I knew that working with her was going to be beneficial to my recovery. She was constantly thinking outside of the box of traditional therapy and doing her research on spinal cord injuries between sessions to help me. Andrea worked on my balance, muscle strengthening, and endurance, always testing my physical abilities and, just as importantly, my sense of humor. She constantly made me laugh, which made the length of therapy so much more enjoyable. I told her she had the perfect personality to intertwine with mine as week after week, month after month, she helped me to make small gains.

After many months of working together and talking about doing therapy "outside of the box," she took me on walks outside of the therapy room. Andrea took me outside of the hospital and had me walk up a hill and she walked right beside me. We walked up and down hospital steps and through countless hospital hallways. She was never afraid to push for medical equipment I needed even when it was outside of the scope of her department's coverage. She made sure that I had what I needed to ensure that I had the fullest possible recovery level.

These different techniques Andrea used were tied to goals I had set for myself.

Trust is a strong word because it has big implications. Andrea gained my trust through her actions. She also gained my friendship, which was cemented through the next few years during our time working together. Andrea and I spoke about many things including family, life, and heartaches amongst other topics, but all our conversations eventually came back to the joy of laughter. We understood that about one another. We both valued the importance of humor to help you through many of life's difficult situations.

Now, I needed to figure out how navigating the pool and changing out of wet clothes into dry clothes after my session would be feasible. This was not possible for me to do for myself with truly little arm and hand function. Rhonda and I figured out those details helped by my nursing assistants.

Managing those details was not my tallest hurdle to get over with aquatic therapy. I soon realized there was an underlying fear of entering the pool. I certainly wasn't expecting that to happen because of my love to be in and around water, but there it was.

The day had arrived for my first aquatic therapy session. I stood back from the edge of the pool, looking at the water with much trepidation. Coming so close to death by way of drowning made this step difficult to navigate in my brain. I was fortunate to have Barry, my pool therapist, to assure me he would not leave my side. He knew my story. He understood my hesitation.

Barry introduced me to a whole new world of therapy I quickly embraced. The warm water helped loosen my tense body and allowed for much easier movement. I've been extremely fortunate to have had knowledgeable therapists that are kind and caring, Barry was no different. It also helped he had a true love for baseball and laughing. Pool, talking baseball and laughing, what's not to like about that?

We started aquatic therapy slowly with me grabbing and holding onto a metal railing, moving one leg or arm at a time, pushing through the water. The water naturally resisted my movements. The railing separated the pool into two sections, the shallow side for walking and a deep side for many other uses.

It wasn't long into our sessions, Barry had me walking from one end of the pool to the other. It wasn't graceful but having that function to stand and move my legs and being in the water helped me improve upon my balance.

To keep therapy from being repetitive, Barry changed the routine, adding what looked like hand weights that you curled to build muscle. These were made from foam, plastic and very lightweight, helping to build strength by water resistance. Swinging my arms with these weights in the water created the resistance helping me strengthen my arms, back and core muscles. I didn't become a Mr. Atlas the bodybuilder, but it did help me regain some strength I would not have had without this therapy.

There were many aquatic exercises and therapies Barry tried with me that helped in ways I wouldn't realize until much later. However, there was one in particular that made an instant impact on my body. Barry wrapped a floatation device around my upper torso and had me lean back into the water as he grabbed me by my ankles. He lifted my legs to the top surface of the water until I was floating on my back. Starting at one end of the pool, Barry would slink my body back and forth like a snake until he reached the other end of the pool. He would repeat this for ten minutes, usually ending our session. This therapy instantly relieved the pressure and pain I was experiencing in my back.

My outpatient treatment helped me maintain the physical gains that I had made in the eleven months since my injury. I had physical therapy, occupational therapy, and pool therapy for the next two years. Eventually, I was able to stay at home alone during the day when Rhonda was at work. Staying alone was an accomplishment that really had not seemed possible. These remarkable therapists helped me achieve the many goals I set for myself through many trials and epic fails. Not all my therapy was difficult, and I looked forward to each session partially for the human interaction.

At this point of recovery, I put extreme focus on the next toughest functional goal to attain. This was to regain enough mobility in my arms and hands that I may recoup the ability to drive. I had gone through an extensive evaluation from MetroHealth's driver rehabilitation and failed. I was fairly disappointed but not deterred since this was on my mind constantly. The memory of losing my truck due to my injury was definitely behind this strong desire to get back the freedom that comes with driving.

I discussed my thoughts with Andrea to work on arm and hand motions to mimic those used to turn a steering wheel in a vehicle. She had an idea! Andrea set up a wheel attachment on a piece of therapy equipment called a BTE (Baltimore Therapeutic Equipment.) It was a PrimusRS. This machine could adjust resistance and calculate your progression over time, among many other functions. It was perfect for giving me resistance, helping rebuild strength in my arms as I turned the wheel. With the wheel being small in thickness, Andrea had to wrap it with material, replicating a vehicle's steering wheel's size and feel. Although this function was difficult and taxing on my arms, I worked on this every session.

About a year had passed since my last driver evaluation, I was feeling confident to schedule another one. Again, I failed. Now I was more frustrated than disappointed. My evaluator did see a significant improvement and had a few suggestions for me to work on. By this time, I was finished with therapy but continued to work on arm stretches and movements at home. I had to think outside the box.

A great friend of ours, Jenna, is a physical therapist so I asked her if she would work with me to help with my deficiencies. She agreed and we set-up a weekly schedule. I was thrilled because she possesses incredible skills, and a happy, bubbly attitude. After evaluating me, Jenna had a game plan. She understood the pushback of my arms and my injury. Jenna and I worked together on my posture, core strengthening and extensively on my arms' range of motion. I understand my arms and hands will never function the way they once did, I just needed a little more range to drive. Five months into this therapy, we decided to start practicing my driving.

I borrowed a spinner knob from a friend of mine and had another friend attach it to our van's steering wheel. It's a device I would need now to practice and later if this process were to work. Jenna took me to the high school near my home where I first taught both of my children to drive. I figured it was the safest place for everyone's sake. Before any of our driving excursions, Jenna would stretch my hands and arms to loosen them. It didn't take long before I felt comfortable enough to venture away from the school parking lot's safe environment to some of the rural roads near home. That turned into much longer drives and in high traffic areas. I was ready.

I called and scheduled my next evaluation, hoping that the third time would be the charm. It was! My evaluator named Mike was happy to see that I hadn't given up and impressed with my progress. He would still need to give me training to get me ready for the state test. Although I understood the need, this was more money leaving my pocket. Mike proved the next few weeks of training were necessary. With his help, I was certified by the state of Ohio. Woohoo!

How do you endure this much therapy for this many years? Attitude and a willingness to try as well as humor! It doesn't hurt to have caring and talented friends and therapists like Kevin, Andrea, Barry, Jenna and the many other therapists who helped me along the way. More friendships and lasting relationships were forged through it all, and they will forever be etched in my memories.

One of the ways we have maintained relationships has been through staying connected to our spinal cord injury community. The United Spinal Association Northeast Ohio Chapter in Cleveland, Ohio (USANEO), helped us both with the emotional side of our transition.

Through USANEO, we became aware of an opportunity to become Peer Mentors for the Christopher and Dana Reeve Foundation Peer and Family Support Program. Rhonda and I completed the training and became members of the first group of certified mentors in Ohio. The Peer Mentor Program provided a way for me to reach out in a meaningful way. The Peer Mentor program has given me a rewarding sense of purpose, which I thought would be lost forever right after the accident. I have always made myself available to help people, but after my time at MetroHealth, I was compelled to seek ways I could help this special population of people. I knew how valuable my interactions were with my friends with similar injuries. We shared specific experiences and having a common understanding was critical to not feeling alone. The Peer Mentor Program gave me the structure to reach out to people who could otherwise be isolated.

One of my most interesting Peer Mentor relationships came in a very unusual way. While I was still at the post-acute rehab facility, my occupational therapist came to our home and educated us about the modifications that would need to be made to our house for me to go home. We interviewed contractors and finally hired someone to do the remodel. Unfortunately, after three months of work, he was nowhere close to finishing, and we had no choice but to fire him. Our house was a disaster and the sheer amount of construction debris rendered it almost unlivable.

We had to start interviewing contractors all over again, but it was difficult to find a company willing to complete another business's unfinished job. We were very frustrated because this would prevent me from going home when I was ready. On one of the days that Rhonda brought me home from the post-acute rehab facility to interview yet another contractor, one of our neighbors happened to stop by the house. Ed had heard the news of my accident and came to our home to ask about me. We shared our nightmare construction story with him, and it just so happened that Ed is a contractor, building custom homes in our area. His company rarely dabbled in remodels, but he had a small crew he thought would be perfect for the job. We signed a contract and work began right away. He turned out to be a godsend.

After a few weeks of construction, I went home for an afternoon visit, and I met the four-man Amish carpenter crew. They stopped to sit and talk with me on their break. They were interested and listened intently to my story. They told me they, along with their church, had been praying for me since starting the project. I was so humbled, and I enjoyed talking to them each time I visited the house during the construction process. Their work was impeccable, allowing me to safely move into our house when I was discharged.

A year and a half after I came home, Rhonda and I decided we wanted an accessible deck off the back of the house, and we called our neighbor Ed, the contractor, to do the work for us. He sent the same four-man crew to our house. They were amazed at the progress I had made because the last time they saw me, I was using a wheelchair full time and now I was walking, albeit awkwardly. I shared with them that I had begun mentoring other people with spinal cord injuries and how encouraging it was for all parties involved. During our talk, one of the men told me about his friend, Daniel, who had suffered a work-related spinal cord injury just six months prior, and he asked me if I would be willing to talk to him.

I was honored and excited for another opportunity to reach out. I was surprised that he gave me his friend's number because most Amish people do not use phones. Later, I learned that some

Amish families are allowed to use phones in special circumstances, and this was certainly a special circumstance.

I called Daniel that night and explained who I was and the reason for my call. We started getting to know each other and I told him he wasn't alone and that I could be a person he and his family could rely on for support. It was such a great first interaction because he was open to talking with me and had many questions that I could answer. I called a few times in the following months to check in with him and we continued to grow close. After a few months, I asked Daniel if he would like a home visit, and he agreed without hesitation.

When Rhonda and I arrived, Daniel, his wife, and their ten children greeted us along with many other relatives, friends, and family as we followed them to their back porch. It was a great night of sharing. Our mentoring relationship with Daniel and his family has enriched our lives and we have grown to love them, enjoying many times of fellowship with the entire community. They have been able to learn from us, but more importantly, we have learned from them. This would never have happened for our two families to meet, and even though the circumstances were because of the injury, we are thankful for the relationship.

Building relationships with all the people I have mentored, blesses me beyond what I could ever have imagined. The opportunity to share our lives, our stories, and our hearts is a gift.

I have also had opportunities to speak to various groups of

people in churches, schools, universities, and healthcare facilities. Before my accident, I was not as sensitive to the need for accessible facilities and the importance of awareness in the community. Now I notice and advocate for necessary changes. I was never comfortable speaking in public, but I realized after the accident it is important to be a voice for other people struggling with a disability and a voice of hope for all. I have developed an awareness that everyone has struggles, whether the struggle is visible, like mine or not.

CHAPTER 14
Calmer Waters

People often ask me what my plans are for the future, and it constantly reminds me how much I am focused on living in the present. I am not compelled to plan for some future thing because I have learned to be more present and in the moment. As I worked on this book and reflected on my life, I realized how much Rhonda and I have overcome and how grateful I am for every part of the journey.

The lessons I learned as a child and young adult gave me the wisdom to trust God and myself. I could see that I can be a voice of encouragement for other people and that my whole story needs to be told. This way, I can possibly be a light in the darkness for someone else. We all have our individual paths, and sometimes it can feel overwhelming to stay on the path. Sometimes it seems that there is no way to see through our difficulties in life. The waves can be so tall and raging that you cannot see the other shore, and there seems to be no way you can get to the other side. Sometimes the journey seems lonely and impossible. I opened up with the truth of my life so my fellow travelers can feel a little bit less alone.

I've been asked if I ever say, "Why me?" and the answer is "Yes." As I shared earlier, I do say *why me* but in a different way than you would think. I say, "Why do I have this level of recovery when so many of my friends in the spinal cord community have not had this amount of regained function?" We don't get answers to those types of questions. I do not take my recovery for granted, and I am humbled and grateful for everything I have regained.

I have come a long way, no denying it. I will be okay mentally, but I will never be "OKAY." So much has been taken away that I can never get back, such as time itself. The physical and mental anguish have taken a toll, not just on me but also on Rhonda and my family. I will forever deal with the daily struggles that come with a spinal cord injury, including the physical and the mental issues like anger, frustration, longing, and uncertainty, but I will continue to hold onto hope. I will keep pushing forward, knowing there will be many obstacles ahead of me. Life as we know it is short and can be very fragile, so I desire to live my life not looking back going through the what-ifs — what if I would have done something differently?

That part of my life is gone and is now a distant memory. I want to live purposefully by finding joy where I can, by experiencing the beauty of this world and all it has to offer. I will continue to cultivate meaningful relationships with the people in my life and look for opportunities to impact lives. No matter how much time remains in my life, I pray that I will serve others in any way that is possible for me.

I have felt the support from family, friends, and complete strangers through their actions and kind words, but many do not understand what it took physically or mentally to get to the point where I am now. People often ask, "How are you doing?" and may hear me tell of the hardships I continue to endure. Their response is normally the same, "Yes, but look how far you have come," or "You are so lucky to be alive." This is hard for me to hear repeatedly because no one knows more about how far I have come or how lucky I am to be alive than me. I do realize their hearts are in the right place and they have the best intentions, but I feel compelled to share this poem to help readers understand why I feel their response has the opposite effect rather than how it is intended.

Don't Call Me Lucky

by Dorothy Mercer

I live with my injuries.
People say to me, "Aren't you lucky!"
And they don't understand
Why my face suddenly freezes
And my voice becomes tense.

I can say I'm lucky
If I so choose on any given day.
But when others say it,
I feel as if
They discount my pain
And don't recognize my costs.
Count me only as alive or dead
No matter how hard it may be

To endure living.

Some days I am glad:
Life itself is all that matters,
And I savor it.

But when I hurt too much,
Or am told I won't fully heal,
When I cannot work or play as before,
Or feel I'm a burden on others,
Then I don't feel lucky at all!
I feel cheated!

Some days I even wish
I had died rather than live like this.
So please don't tell me
That I'm lucky
To only be injured.

Tell me instead
You are glad I'm still here.
And let me know why.
Tell me that you care about
My grief, pain, anger, and adjustments. Tell me you
Willingly rehear
My disappointments, loss, and frustrations.
And have patience while I relearn to live.

Then someday I can tell you
How lucky I am – to have someone
Who understands and accepts my sorrows
And who also
shares my joys!

I have gained so much knowledge through my own healing process and others who have suffered a spinal cord injury sharing their journeys with me. I hope Dorothy Mercer's poem will help my readers see into her heart and the hearts of so many of us working each day to survive.

As I look to the future, I feel deeply grateful for the people who were and are with me and keep me from giving up. I look forward to spending time with them and all the new people I will meet as we move through this life. I am extremely glad that my buddy pulled me out of that water. In many ways, I feel more alive now than I ever have because of the things I have learned on this journey.

My life reminds me of my favorite movie, *The Sandlot*. If you don't know the movie, the story is set in a neighborhood full of young boys who get together every day and play baseball. Their lives are consumed with baseball. They are bonded by it. My childhood resembled that movie in so many ways. When I played baseball, I felt like everything was right in the world. In my mind, I wanted to play forever, even though knowing there would be a time when this might not physically be possible. There is an old saying, "nothing lasts forever," and that day came when I didn't feel thoroughly disappointed if a game was rained out or canceled for some other reason. WHAT? This had never happened before. I knew something was different. I knew my playing days in competitive baseball were drawing near to the end. I didn't love the game any less than I did when I was a little boy. I loved it the same, but I realized that I no longer had the skills to compete at the high level that I expected of myself, so I stepped away. My last season was in the fall before my spinal cord injury. There was no opportunity to change my mind.

I'm fortunate I do not feel the same way about my life. If I judged my life as I judged playing baseball, I may have wanted to step away and give up. I can no longer function at the high level I always had after the accident. I cannot go to work, remodel rooms in my house, landscape my yard, or participate in sports. If I had allowed my old way of perceiving life — my worth based on performance — then I might have refused to see so many opportunities. The day Rhonda told me she wasn't leaving, and I realized I could still have purpose, things shifted. I chose to stay in the game. My old way of thinking might have caused me to quit, knowing I had diminished abilities and my function could not be the same. I realized life is not a game, and I'm not willing to just step away from it no matter how much my skill levels deteriorate. After all, this is life, which is precious and cannot be taken lightly. A dollar bill has the same value no matter how it appears on the surface. We all have value, and our lives are worth living.

So, my plans for the future are to live. Life is precious, so I'm living it to the fullest. We have one shot at life on earth, so I live it knowing I'm not guaranteed tomorrow. One of my friends shared the idea that the present will be your actual gift if you are present-focused. She is right. I feel we all can experience a full life. We go through the motions, daily routines and often don't stop to really feel the moment. We don't understand the moment like I do now. Every moment is important to me, and my message is that it can be for you, too.

Life sometimes takes all that we have, causing us to dig deep, deep within our heart, mind, and soul to survive. I hope that my story will be about much more than just me. I hope my story touches every person who suffers, whether they are affected by a spinal cord injury, heart issues, divorce, mental illness, abuse, losing a loved one, or anything that breaks the heart. I feel more broken physically than ever, yet I have never felt more alive. May the broken parts in you heal and make you stronger than you could have ever imagined.

These experiences, thoughts, and how I coped with life in this book are my personal journey. I have spoken with many people who have gone through tremendous hardships and they have had different reactions and outcomes than I have had. We all see our hardships differently and we all react differently. One of the beauties of life is that we are all individuals. We know we are human. We each get to navigate the waves of our own experience. I hope that my journey will help you to navigate your personal waves and find your way into calmer waters.

I'd like to leave you with two quotes that have meant a lot to me.

Dreams

"So many of our dreams at first seem impossible, then they seem improbable, and then when we summon the will, they soon become inevitable."

– Christopher Reeve

Defining Moments

"When a defining moment comes along, you define the moment, or the moment defines you."

– Kevin Costner

ABOUT THE AUTHOR

John and Rhonda Chartier

John Chartier is the definition of a Jack-of-all-trades. His career has taken him from construction to the automotive industry then to quality in manufacturing and now to writing his memoir. Who would have thought a book idea would materialize from lying in a hospital bed back in May of 2013? It did!

Married to Rhonda for over 37 years, the couple has two brilliant children, Brandon and Jordyn, thanks in part to Rhonda being the amazing teacher she is. John enjoys spending time with his two dogs, Maizie and Beaux, and cat, Cosmo. John also enjoys taking in a baseball game whenever possible. Living in a sleepy little town in Northeast Ohio has allowed John to write and finish this book in...seven *years*. Stay tuned, who knows what could happen in the next seven?

CPSIA information can be obtained
at www.ICGtesting.com
Printed in the USA
BVHW050706290522
638400BV00020B/501